Small

MW01127252

A Bohemian Woman's Story of Survival

Dear Jeanie + Tom,
It's such a joy sending this book
to you. Hope it's meaningful &
interesting. Love, Sylvia 12/6/05

Sylvia Welner and
Kevin Welner

Hello Jean,
Isn't it nice to know that
those nursery school lessons finally
paid off. Who'da thought I could
write! Best wishes + happy reading.
Kevin

Hamilton Books
A member of
The Rowman & Littlefield Publishing Group, Inc.
Lanham · Boulder · New York · Toronto · Oxford

Copyright © 2005 by
Hamilton Books
4501 Forbes Boulevard
Suite 200
Lanham, Maryland 20706
UPA Acquisitions Department (301) 459-3366

PO Box 317
Oxford
OX2 9RU, UK

Library of Congress Control Number: 2005929327
ISBN 0-7618-3258-0 (paperback : alk. ppr.)

DEDICATION

This book is dedicated to Jaroslav, without whose patient, thoughtful assistance this book could not have been written.

TABLE OF CONTENTS

PREFACE

For most of the twentieth century, Czechs lived under a succession of external rulers. Up until the end of World War I, what is now the Czech Republic was part of the Austro-Hungarian Empire. The Czech people suffered as pawns through two world wars and German and Russian occupations. Derek Sayer in *The Coasts of Bohemia* writes, "In reality Bohemia has been a frontier zone, over which armies of competing modernities—Reformation and Counter-Reformation, empire and nation, fascism and democracy, capitalism and communism—have repeatedly rolled back and forth."[1] This historical pattern provides the broad context for this book, as Tonča (pronounced *Tone'-cha*) matter-of-factly tells of her daily life.

When Tonča's son, Jaroslav, at age forty-four, emigrated to America in 1969, Tonča began sending him letters. At that time, she was sixty-four years old. Sixteen years later, at her son's request, Tonča started to jot down her memories which she included in her letters to him. She continued to insert these memories on and off up to the age of ninety-one. Jaroslav, or *Jára* (pronounced *Ya´-ra*) as his mother called him, had lacked curiosity about his mother's earlier life when he was younger; but in his more mature years, he became more interested. Although Tonča left school during the fourth grade, she educated herself by reading books throughout her adulthood—an education that is evident in her correspondence. Her letters show a level of detail and care (they include no erasures or cross-outs) demonstrating exceptional mental acuity, even in her old age. At the time of this book's writing, she was ninety-five years old and living in a nursing home in the Czech Republic.

Tonča's letters render a picture of village life in early 20th century Czechoslovakia. They are presented here as memoirs reflecting the society of the day—the values, attitudes, prejudices, and assumptions arising out of the harsh lives of Tonča and her neighbors. Tonča usually began her letters offering thoughts having little general interest, such as *I'm feeling a little better than last time I wrote you*. Such comments are not included among the passages reproduced in this book, which instead focuses on her memories of earlier times. Although she was in her eighties and nineties when she wrote most of these letters, her mind was sound and her memories often quite detailed. That said, however, the original letters do not offer a tightly woven narrative. They are instead presented as a series of quick snapshots of her earlier life. By reorganizing the letters into chapters presented chronologically, we have attempted to build coherence, and to highlight details, themes, and anecdotes. Because Tonča is chatting with her son, her original letters often omit explanations and details. Therefore, we have added a few clarifications in short passages, shown in brackets, as well as subheadings within the chapters, for the purpose of tying together Tonča's correspondence.

This adaptation of Tonča's letters into book format endeavors to preserve the original meaning, idiom, and narrative style of her letters. However, given the idiosyncracies of a translation from Czech to English, we have also taken the liberty of making some changes in grammar and syntax. For authenticity, Czech names of places (such as *Praha* for Prague) are preserved as well as the Czech language convention of change of gender for female names expressed through the ending *ová* or *á* (example: *Vitáková and Hrubá* from the male names *Viták and Hrubý*). For ease of reading, this book uses the English language convention *"s"* to pluralize names and *" 's"* to show possession (example: *the Vitáks* and *Vitáková's*) instead of the Czech language conventions.

Several themes emerge from Tonča's memoirs. They typify conditions in Central Europe during the period covered in her letters, conditions interwoven into the fabric of Tonča's life and those around her. Several of her stories, for instance, demonstrate that survival was the cornerstone of marriage for the poor in Bohemia. Also, death repeatedly arises as a commonplace occurrence that permeates everyday existence—experienced and endured in a way that will seem strange to most of today's readers. Tonča's knowledge, beliefs and experiences are natural to her and she presents them as such. Her letters show how human beings find meaning even amid a life of severe hardships and dangers. Patricia Hampl in her memoir, *A Romantic Education,* writes about how the Czech people managed to adapt and survive among these conditions: "One does not *live* in such a situation; one lives *as if* everything were all right, as if everything were normal."[2] Each of Tonča's letters is preceded by a segment entitled, 'Jára's background notes,' which reflects on these and other themes. Jára's notes also provide contextual information, placing his mother's narratives within the historical, social, economical and cultural framework of the particular period. In the final chapter, Jára shares some personal information that tells how and why he and his mother became geographically separated. That chapter and introductory Notes are adapted from one-on-one interviews with Jára. At the end of the book is an appendix with an historical time line, family trees, and sketched maps of the areas Tonča discusses.

ACKNOWLEDGMENTS

Tonča, I know you couldn't imagine yourself as the central character of a book or realize the remarkable nature of what to you was a simple, ordinary life. You and I never met, but I have come to know you as a dear friend. Your letters touched me profoundly with their power to dissolve the barriers of distance and time, culture and circumstance.

Jára, I treasure what you have shared with me. You have made your mother's letters accessible to me through your translations and explanations of the Czech culture. Although it was not within our original plan, you became a storyteller too. I know it wasn't easy for you to talk about some of your most intimate feelings, especially concerning times of anguish and intense frustrations.

Blanka, thank you for your contributions, both comments and ideas. The addition of your observations and perspective provided a wonderful spiritual richness.

To my son, Kevin, and husband, Jerry, a special thanks for their continuous enthusiasm and support throughout the development of this project. Finally, a heartfelt thanks to friends and family who read and offered editorial comment on the many drafts of this book: Ceeroosh Hartunian, Virginia Hartunian, Abbe Scones, Cindy Todd, Alison Vredenburgh, Don Weitzman, and Judy Wilson.

Sylvia Welner
Los Angeles, California
January, 2005

**"It hurts more when
no one knows your pain."**

Czech proverb

TONČA'S LETTERS

Chapter 1
Our Cottage Near the Creek

Jára's background notes
Rovensko, 1905-1917 (Austro-Hungarian Empire up through World War I)

Mother's letters describe a life where courts and government rarely touched the lives of the average person. Rovensko, where Mother lived as a child, was a small town, more like a village, really. The same families lived together in the same area often over a period of several generations. This resulted in a community where neighbors' opinions had a widespread and strong effect, as illustrated in the following letter when my mother discusses how her family honored a commitment that became unexpectedly burdensome.

When Mother was a little girl, she and her family were considered peasants. Formally, the feudal system had ended, but Bohemian poor were still economically dependent on the landowner class for menial jobs to supplement their meager income. Before the Industrial Age, most Czech people were farmers or performed other manual labor. All family members began contributing to the family's survival as soon as they passed the toddler stage.

Early manufacturing was done at home. Small factories developed little by little, but most production still depended on traditional manual labor methods. Moreover, the simple factory machinery that existed at that time was generally hard to use and dangerous for the workers.

Traditionally, the people of Rovensko, where my grandparents lived, made a living in the piecework, home-based jewelry business. Yet this small town could not provide enough work to support the community. For more opportunities, many of the locals, like my grandfather and aunts, found jobs in cities of Jičín or Jablonec, about twenty miles away. If their jobs turned out to be permanent, they often relocated in order to avoid the long train commute.

Mother describes in some detail her memories that center around food. Particularly during the First World War and more generally during her childhood, food was a basic concern and the only affordable way to enhance a holiday or family event.

Here's what my mother had to say about Rovensko and her early childhood.

Tonča's letter to Jára

I'm glad that you suggested that I write about my life. It has helped me to stop thinking about my aches and pains and given me a new interest—a way to fill my days and break the monotony of my daily routine.

As you know, I grew up in a one-room cottage in the village of Rovensko. When my parents bought our place, the sellers let them have it for less than the asking price. But there was one catch. Our family had to allow their *Babička* [grandmother] to stay on with us after they moved out.

In this way, Babička became a rent-free boarder in our tiny cottage. The agreement made my parents responsible for providing living space and food to a total stranger for the rest of her life. Of course, they thought that the old woman would die soon. She was in failing health, exhausted from a life of hard work. But her condition changed completely when she no longer had to work. She perked up and was full of energy. Instead of wasting away and dying, she lived twenty-two more years. During that time, without fail, we gave the old woman her rations: a half-liter of milk daily, a quarter-pound of butter per week, cottage cheese, potatoes, eggs, and fruit.

During the first twelve years, Babička lived with us in the one room where we all ate and slept. Like the rest of us, she slept on the floor on a straw mattress. Our family continued to grow, and after the number of children reached five, the noise became more than she could bear. Babička couldn't sleep at night, and in the morning she was grumpy and tired. She cried, "I have to get out of here." Fortunately, one of the old woman's daughters lived in the same village, and she agreed to let her mother move in with her. Although Babička chose not to live with us any longer, we continued to fulfill our duty to feed her. Either I or one of my sisters carried the ration of food to her at her daughter's place. It was a lot of extra work for us, and we didn't like it one bit.

In the early years, our family owned a cow, so the milk, butter and cheese came from our supply. This changed when my mother became ill. We sold the cow because we could no longer afford to keep it. After that, we had to buy these foods for the old woman. We were unhappy about the expense, but that didn't stop us from keeping our word. During the next ten years, we kept our promise even though we barely had enough money and food for our own survival.

When she knew she was going to die, Babička asked me to take a message to my mother. In the message she begged in God's name for forgiveness for all the inconvenience she caused our family. On hearing the news of her death, my mother, a devout Catholic, exclaimed, "Our Heavenly Father has freed us at last!"

Living near the creek

The creek that flowed by our cottage played a big part in our lives. It was a piece of the shortcut we children made to reach the railroad tracks where we liked to play. We found it was much faster and more fun to run down the hillside and wade through the creek than to follow the regular path the adults took. From bank to bank, the creek was about six feet across. Usually there was no more than one foot of water in it, though some spots were deeper because the bottom was uneven, with unexpected holes.

The small stream had other uses that were important to the community. My parents depended on it for watering our small potato patch. The women of Rovensko washed their laundry and bathed in it. Some small fish lived in the water, but we never thought of catching them. Fish were not part of our regular diet. We lived far from the sea or any inland body of water where fish were plentiful. In those days before trucks, trains and refrigeration, people ate only what was available locally.

Although the creek water looked clear, we didn't drink it. For our drinking water, we had to go to a pump three houses down the hill. All of our neighbors went there for their water. This wasn't a problem in summer, but in winter the path to the pump was icy and dangerously slippery. Later, the people of the village put in a well near the road with a built-in pump; that was a great improvement for us. Unfortunately, by that time I was grown and lived away from home.

Most of my memories of the creek are happy, but there are a few exceptions—like the day the creek overflowed. It didn't just over run its banks. The water flooded an area that was about three hundred feet wide! My mother was working in our potato patch and I was sitting on the ground nearby when we were suddenly caught in a huge downpour. My mother quickly tossed me up onto her back and ran towards our cottage. At three and a half, I was old enough to wrap my arms around her neck and hold on tightly, my little legs clutching her waist.

In a minute, Mother and I were drenched. The rain that started from a small cloud had grown into a raging storm. It didn't take long for the water in the creek to rise to the top of its banks and pour out over the countryside. The mill that stood at the bottom of the hill soon was covered up to the second floor. People said they didn't remember the creek ever flooding like this before.

The creek was real, but for me, it was also something magical. I loved to play by the edge of the stream and lose myself in thought. Sitting and watching the water flow, I wondered where it was going. Did the water come up from the ground, and when the level dropped was it because it got sucked back in? If I fell in the creek, would I die or be carried to some strange place? Would I be taken back to God? Even when I was young, death was more a curiosity than something scary.

My mother always told me not to go too close to the creek, but I didn't listen. None of us knew how to swim because the creek was for wading, not swimming. (Jára, it wasn't until you children were grown that I learned to swim.) Once, I was standing close to the water's edge holding tightly to a birch tree branch. Suddenly, for some reason, I let go. My mother was washing the laundry in the creek when she heard the splash. "Tonča! Tonča!" she yelled. When I didn't answer, she ran frantically to look for me in the water. Seeing me, she reached out and pulled me to the bank with her last strength. Fortunately, a neighbor was just walking by. She saw what had happened, and immediately went into action. "Help me. We have to flip Tonča upside down," she ordered. "Be quick! She probably swallowed a lot of water." Mother did the best she could. It was my neighbor who provided the strength. I was unconscious and didn't wake up until much later, in my own bed. Even when I opened my eyes, I couldn't remember anything that had happened.

Remembering the creek also brings to mind an incident that occurred when I was just four years old. On that day, I was walking along the part of the creek where women from Rovensko frequently bathed. A group of them were there that day, some of them in smocks, but most of them were completely naked. I stared in awe. I knew that I wasn't the only one watching because I saw a man peeking out from behind the bushes. He was a little man with a sharp nose. When he noticed that I saw him, he must have run off because he disappeared among the trees. I didn't recognize him and never saw him again. How strange! Where did he come from? Not from our village or I would've recognized him—if not then, later on.

Playing on the railroad tracks

As a young child, I liked to play with the pretty little white pebbles scattered along the railroad tracks near our home. I remember one time sitting among the pebbles not far from some older children who were rambling along the tracks. Suddenly, we all heard a sound in the distance. The other children knew it was a train whistle. (Honestly, I must have known, too.) Off they ran, leaving me behind. The trainman blasted a warning, but I just didn't understand the danger. The train kept coming. I stood there frozen, my feet stuck to the spot. In what seemed to me the very last second, the train screeched to a halt. The conductor climbed down angrily from the engine car and walked straight towards me. I had no idea what he was going to do to me. My knees were quivering, but I still didn't move. Glaring down at me, the conductor picked me up and shook me violently. Then he set me on the grass, and gave me a push down the hillside. His powerful hand hurt me, but I was glad to be far away from his scowling face.

In spite of that close call, it wasn't the last time I played on the tracks. My parents didn't like it, but they didn't let it worry them either. We were always outside. Our one-room cottage was only for sleeping and eating. Once I walked out the door, everything I saw was mine to explore. We had no fenced-in yard, no real limits as to how far I could wander, except my mother expected me to be close enough to hear in case she called. Sometimes, when I knew she didn't need me, I took a walk into the nearby woods and collected mushrooms and berries with the older children.

But when I was very young, the railroad was a special attraction. I liked the loud whistle and the sound of the train rushing by. Since it passed only twice a day, the tracks were usually a quiet place where I could sit peacefully examining the shiny little pebbles. We didn't have any signals or other warnings at railroad crossings in the Rovensko area. Danger was something you were supposed to notice for yourself by using your eyes and ears. Our parents knew that children often ignored risks until the last minute. Adults weren't much better. Taking chances, hoping for the best, was how we moved from one moment to the next. It wasn't that we didn't care about dying. It's that everyday life was full of hazards, and so we developed a fearless if not careless attitude about familiar dangers.

Evil spirits

I was born on Easter Sunday. This convinced my mother that I possessed innate miraculous powers. When my sister, Anča, bruised her hand, Mother asked me to exorcize the evil spirit from her body. To please her, I chanted the incantation: "I, sorceress of God, will help as I can and what I can't help, I leave to God."

In our minds, evil spirits might decide to appear anywhere, anytime. Their power was enormous and could only be challenged by God Himself. We believed that both God and spirits could send us signs or omens. Both were real to us and so we treated all evidence of the spiritual world with respect and awe. God we knew as a stern, shadowy figure who lived in churches and insisted that we conform to His set of absolute rules. But except for Mother, who was truly religious, we were most occupied with the evil spirits who had the greatest hold over us. They lived in our homes and in the places where we played, like Trosky Ruins, where the old [Gothic] castle once stood. Pesky as these spirits were, they were our intimate companions, trailing along like unwanted kid sisters, demanding our attention and threatening to tattle if they didn't get their way.

My brother, Pepa, was still a boy when he was snatched from us. The only memories I have of him were from when I was four years old and he was twelve. My sisters had covered me up with a pile of autumn leaves; Pepa dug me out. That same year, he went on a day trip with his schoolmates to Trosky Ruins. As soon as he arrived home, he ran breathlessly into the house and gulped down several large cups of water. Several days later, he became very sick and a short time later, lost his sight. Right before he died, God gave us a sign. On the wall, we had a shelf held in place by a piece of string. Without warning, it broke as if someone clipped it neatly in half. The shelf and all its contents fell clattering to the floor. My mother said, "The breaking of the string was a sign warning us of his death."

Another strange thing happened before Pepa died. One night, I was standing at the window in the attic when I was surprised by a strange sight. The sky suddenly lit up as if it were daytime. The brightness lasted only for a few seconds. (Much later, I learned the light was probably from a meteor with a long tail.) Why do I remember it today? Maybe it's because the head pointed toward Trosky Ruins, which was known to be a haunted place. We children used to stare upward at the cliffs and wonder if there were evil spirits hiding there. We half expected them to appear suddenly, swoop down, and carry us away. Nothing scary happened to us girls, but afterwards I had the thought that perhaps the bright light was another omen warning that Pepa would soon be taken from us. I never told Mother what I suspected.

When a family member died in our tiny house, we had to remove the front window to lower the coffin through the opening. That was because our house was built on a slope making the front door at the second floor level. (The ground level was the goat shed.) Coming out the door, you had to walk down some steep narrow stairs made of stones now worn uneven with age. It would be dangerous to carry a coffin down such stairs. After Pepa died, our family carried the empty coffin in and later lifted him out through the front window. In those days, the windows were hinged and easily removable. Until the coffin was ready, which took three or four days, Pepa's body remained laid out on the table with flowers by his head and candles at his feet.

Because I was so young when Pepa died, his death was more of a curiosity than a tragedy to me. Truly, I was more touched by the activities surrounding his death, his coffin and burial, than his actual passing. Now, as I look back, I can feel the pain as a mother that I was unable to feel as a little sister. Pepa was my parents' only son. Fortunately, God had given Mother a sign, the broken string. That omen seemed to give her some comfort that God was paying attention and would be looking out for her beloved son in heaven.

Maminka **and** *tatínek*

Our mother and father were known to us affectionately as *maminka* and *tatínek*. *Maminka*, poor thing, how she suffered during her short life. She was only forty-eight when she died. The hillside, where only alfalfa would grow, proved fateful for her. She was tending the crop when she stumbled and fell, rolling all the way down the hill. What made matters worse, she was pregnant at the time and all that bouncing around caused her to have a miscarriage. Mother never recovered her health after that. Before her fall, she had always worked hard. Afterwards, everything changed. The accident, combined with delivering seven babies at home with no assistance, had taken a toll on her body.

Despite delicate health, my mother gave birth again to another girl. I was six, the youngest child in the family, when the baby came. She was born in a hospital in Jičín. *Tatínek* must have been very worried or he wouldn't have brought *maminka* to the hospital; most women delivered at home. As it happened, the infant survived only a few days. Her name was Markétka, and she was the only one of us who had beautiful black hair like my mother.

Before she gave birth to Markétka, *maminka* was able to get around a bit. *Tatínek* made crutches for her so she could see the first villa in Rovensko built right next to the railroad tracks. It belonged to Vrabec, the mayor. I walked with her up to the highway to a spot from where we could get a good view of the villa. That was the last journey my mother made. When she returned home from the hospital after Markétka was born, *maminka* never moved from her bed. When we cleaned the room and changed the linen, we had to lift her out of bed, set her carefully on *tatínek*'s mattress on the floor, and then carry her back to bed again. I cry whenever I think back to those days.

Mother's accident occurred when I was just five years old. It's a pity I remember my mother only as an invalid. She was ill for thirteen years. It was my responsibility to care for her during those years, eight of which she was confined to bed and in great pain. For my mother, I never considered any task a bother. I disposed of her bodily wastes and did it gladly. I rinsed everything away in the creek where it flowed through our garden. Every day, I ran home from school eager to be with her. I bathed her and combed her hair. She had beautiful long black hair and blue eyes. "Your mother was a beauty when she was young," the neighbors used to tell me. "How clean she used to look in the starched cotton apron she always wore. Like a doll."

My poor father didn't have an easy life with her. Nevertheless, he was kind to her. I don't remember that they ever had a quarrel. For years, he slept on a mattress on the floor to give her more room in bed to settle her aching body.

I slept on a straw mattress with Julča; Růža slept with Anča. Sometimes in winter, I wet the mattress. My father, hoping to discourage me from doing it again, spanked me for it.

Maminka was very religious, but God didn't seem to help her in her suffering. Even so, she insisted that all of her children go to church. We didn't have warm clothing so we often returned home shivering and aching. Many times I cried because the cold crept under my fingernails. I am sure, the pain I suffered was the beginning of my impatience with church and religion.

When we were children, *tatínek* clearly liked Julča the best. You would think that I, being the baby of the family, would have been *tatínek*'s favorite. But that wasn't the case. Father was reserved and serious, unlike Julča. It was easy for her to show her affection with a hug and a kiss. None of his other daughters had the courage to show her feelings to him as openly. Julča used to run to *tatínek* when she saw him approaching the house coming home from work. He would pick her up and carry her home in his arms.

But here's what I remember best: one time he brought home someone else's child. Our neighbors had eight kids. One of their little girls was hanging around in front of our house. Not paying attention, he scooped her up and carried her into our house, thinking she was Julča. Then suddenly he noticed Julča standing in back of the room with a pained expression on her face. My mother looked at them both and burst out laughing. I didn't laugh, although I was secretly glad to see the effect *tatínek*'s mistake had on Julča.

Even as a child I slept poorly. I couldn't fall asleep and many times I overheard *maminka* and *tatínek* talking. They talked about what to buy first out of the skimpy salary *tatínek* earned. We always seemed to need bedding and shoes. Because I was the youngest, I had to wear everything handed down from my older sisters. That was to be expected. I never thought I was being mistreated. I understood how hard my parents struggled to keep us fed and clothed. I remember that my sister, Máňa, being the eldest in the family, gave us her entire salary. Poor girl. The lady she worked for would say, "Buy something for yourself. You can't walk in the city dressed so badly."

In summer and in winter

As I remember, we used to get up very early—maybe four in the morning during the summer and five a.m. in the winter. Bedtime was at about nine o'clock. Our evening meal was simple and basic. *Maminka* cooked the food in a single pot, which she also brought to the table. We didn't use plates or silverware. Each of us had our own dipping spoon for scooping up the contents of the pot, mostly liquid. Anything solid, like a piece of carrot or potato, we grabbed with our fingers. I imagine poor families everywhere in Bohemia ate that way.

In winter, when we got home from school, we wanted to run out and go sledding in the snow. But that was out of the question. If we were lucky, maybe we could sled on Sundays. Instead of playing, we had to sit at the table and string beads. We each had our own small pot of ruby red crystals to string.

Actually, our work started before we strung the beads. First, we had to walk to the nearby town of Václaví to get them. The crystals were heavy, so two of us went together. It was a good three-quarters of an hour hike even though we took a shortcut through the forest. Then we often had to wait a long time for the man with the beads to come. We returned very late on those days. Because it was dark, we had to go home the long way through the muddy fields. That route was safer and less spooky, but not without its foulness. Our feet were bare, and the damp, squishy ground sent a chill up our legs when the temperature fell. We arrived home mucky, tired, and hungry. Still, we knew that stringing crystals was not play or simply a child's chore. It was the way we could help our parents supplement the family income.

At that time, many if not most Rovensko families ground and strung garnet stones at home. We children used to help *tatínek* set the stones in a hard wax so they'd be firmly in place for grinding. Using a little wooden stick, wider at one end than the other, one of us pressed wax onto the stick. Then, with great precision, *tatínek* set the garnet into the wax and ground it on a hand grinder. Perhaps *tatínek* didn't have the skill necessary for this type of work, because he stopped doing it after one year. He was used to heavy labor, like chopping wood. Working with tiny garnets was too delicate a work for his calloused hands. Later, a grinding mill was built in Turnov, doing away with the family garnet businesses in Rovensko. The resulting loss of income was an economic disaster for the people of Rovensko.

We children had to do so much! I fed the hungry geese in the backyard shortly after I arrived home from school. I could hear them honking from a distance, but as soon as they saw me, they started to screech with joy. We cared for two or three goats and varying numbers of geese, chickens, and rabbits. Tending the animals was fun. But other chores, like making hay, were not. The goats depended on the hay for food during the winter months, but it was hard work to cut the grass and spread it out to dry.

One spring day, Ladík from the mill was grazing his cattle on the grass near my geese. One of his cows strayed over to the field nearby and gorged herself on tender new clover. Her stomach was accustomed to the winter hay and couldn't digest the green clover. Before Ladík could get her out, she bloated. Ladík ran for help and three men came right away. They cut a hole in one of the cow's stomachs to let out the gas, but it was too late. Ladík should have been more careful. He knew that spring clover gives cows gas. A loss of a cow was costly. His parents had only a few and they depended on its products to help their family survive.

I knew about cows bloating, but I didn't believe that rabbits really do sleep with their eyes open—until I saw it for myself. One afternoon, I was gathering mushrooms in the forest. I saw a hare asleep on the forest floor. Staring at his open eyes, I watched him for awhile, then I grabbed him by the ears. But I guess I wasn't holding tight enough; he slipped out of my hands and ran away.

On my way home, I made my own shortcut, crossing over some deep water and a patch of small thickets. I built a bridge plus a hand support by bending two slender young birch trees. One of them I used to walk on. Holding the bag full of mushrooms that I had collected in one hand, I still had a hand free to hang on to the other tree as I crossed. This is the way it was with me. I was always trying to find some support to hang on to with one hand and still be able to reach out for something better with the other.

Besides picking mushrooms, another task that my sisters and I shared was hauling firewood from the forest. To gather enough firewood, we had to go as far as Vydlák to the pond below Trosky Ruins. We were always on the lookout for the ranger. We knew that he would chase us away if he saw us.

Although it was illegal to take firewood, we rarely gave it a thought. Our only concern was getting caught. The forest was public land to us, a place where we could go to gather, pick, or capture whatever we were lucky enough to find. The fact that the forest was protected land was meaningless since in our eyes it was our backyard. Knowing that the government neither protected nor assisted ordinary people like us, we had little respect for regulations that got in the way of our survival. We didn't break laws to gain riches. We just did what was required to find food and keep ourselves warm.

My father's life of drudgery

Tatínek never stopped working. His life was full of drudgery. During the summer, he went to Jablonec where he made money carrying mortar on his back for bricklayers. (We'd say he was going to "Germans" because mostly German people lived in Jablonec.) There weren't any elevators then; everything had to be carried on ladders. *Tatínek* worked ten hours a day with a heavy barrel óf mortar strapped to his back. Jará, can you imagine that?

On Saturdays, when he came home for the weekend, we used to wait for him at the railroad station in Ktová, which was actually closer to our home than the

Rovensko station. When *tatínek* got off the train, we'd go into the pub next to the station house. He would order a beer and let us lick off the foam. I didn't like the bitter taste, but I relished this private time with my father. These were the rare lighthearted moments we had with *tatínek*. At the pub, we could concentrate on the foam on top of the of beer as if it were the most important thing in our lives. We'd sit there together, nice and cozy, feeling happy to be able to be part of *tatínek's* few personal moments of pleasure.

On Sundays, the trains ran less frequently, but the station was still an active place. Young men and women liked to hang around there to flirt and socialize. When I became the appropriate age to join the group, the train station no longer was the gathering place for such activities. We preferred the pubs where we could go to listen to music, dance, and enjoy a beer. By that time, my tastes had changed.

Jobs my father did to bring in income

In winter, *tatínek* went to "Germans" to cut ice for butchers and innkeepers. They had deep cellars and the ice they stored there lasted all summer. After the beet sugar harvest season, he worked in a sugar factory. During the war [World War I], he and my sister, Julča, found work in a jam factory near the railroad station. But the factory closed the next spring; now there's a dairy on that spot. I also remember *tatínek* working for a company making barrel spigots.

All these jobs were on top of the work *tatínek* had to do inside our house and in our own little field. When the weather was good, he went to the woods to collect branches for firewood. For our crops, he borrowed a plowing horse from a nearby rich farmer (we couldn't afford to have our own horse). In exchange, *tatínek* did some work for the man. After all that labor, *tatínek* went home to sleep on a straw mattress on the floor, my mother having the only bed. She was an invalid for half of the time they had together. Looking back, I marvel at what a hard life he had. But at the time, it all seemed normal. I knew nothing else.

Feeding the family during wartime

When *tatínek* did the cooking, he often made us *kyselo* (sauerkraut cooked in a sour milk and flour mixture) for breakfast. I hated it, but it was a favorite of my father's because it was cheap and easy to prepare. *Maminka* didn't like it either so he added a little butter to her portion, which she usually shared with me. Our evening meal sometimes consisted of barley soaked in milk. When *tatínek* did the cooking, we usually had gruel with plum sauce.

Before the war, on Sundays, we typically had a small amount of beef, usually a half a pound that served the seven of us. We also had castrated goat, which was the cheapest kind of meat and not as smelly as the meat from other goats. Over the winter months, we usually consumed two of these goats. I remember that *tatínek* even had castrated goat at his wedding party when he remarried years later, after *maminka's* death.

We didn't have any meat at all during wartime. But we did have good potatoes and a barrel of kraut that lasted all winter. We also made mashed potato dumplings.

Store-bought food was rationed, but it didn't matter because groceries were almost nonexistent. We relied on tips from neighbors to tell us where and when there might be basic supplies for sale, such as flour or lard. There were lines for everything that became available. Unfortunately, only those people standing in front of the line got what they wanted. I was little, so I got pushed away and returned home empty-handed.

Basically, we grew up on potatoes, beets and carrots. We had a big iron pot of these vegetables simmering all day on the stove. We dipped into the pot whenever we felt hungry. The mill keeper's wife sometimes would call to my mother as she passed by our window, "Drbohlavová, what do you give your children to eat that makes them so healthy and rosy cheeked?" Her children were all pale.

I liked to drop in on the Drahoňovský family who lived near us. They always had potatoes and salt on the table. I would sit there and stuff myself until I couldn't eat any more. The Drahoňovskýs didn't mind. We were neighbors and, like ours, their potatoes were all home grown. They were the color of egg yolks and were delicious with salt. Our custom was to salt each potato, one at a time, just before we popped it into our mouths. Potatoes were actually our staple. During the war, we ate them cold, instead of bread (which was scarce).

Growing potatoes was hard work, and I took over much of that work when Julča, who helped *tatínek* before me, started working in a factory making jam. We used to inherit household jobs, one child after another. I started helping my father with this work when I was about twelve. In the spring, we hauled manure to the field on the hill. My father loaded a wheelbarrow, tied a loop of rope around me, and I pulled. My shoulders got all bruised from the rope. Harvest work was not as bad and had the advantage of taking place on St. Wenceslaus Day when the fair opened in town. We all hurried with our chores so we could visit the fair, at least for a short time.

Fruit was one food that was plentiful. We had fresh fruit in summer and enough apples stored in the attic to last the entire winter. The apples stayed cold under the hay and sometimes even froze during cold winters. If that happened, we didn't mind eating thawed apples; we liked our fruit in any form.

In the summertime, when I woke up in the morning, I couldn't wait to run out and collect pears from our tree. Although the trees were surrounded by swarms of wasps, I don't remember ever being stung. First, I picked any pears that were ripe, and then I ran around to the neighbors' gardens to collect whatever I could find. We were allowed to pick up any fruit that fell to the ground. Nobody minded. Fruit was not sold and sometimes not even picked, like in the Kožený garden. They were old and childless and so didn't have much need for it. Anyway, who would climb their trees? In the fall, I would go back there again, this time collecting nuts.

Sometimes I would sneak into a neighbor's garden to pick some early plums. I'd also be sure to return, a little later in the season, when the plums were ripe and juicy. One neighbor owned a kiln, so the rest of us would bring over piles of fruit. The kiln dried the plums, preserving them so that we would have delicious fruit to eat all year long. The wonderful smell of the drying plums filled the air. Some of the plums burst while drying, so we had to remove them and eat them on the spot. Oh, how good and sweet they tasted!

The Náhlovský family, who lived close to us, had grapevines growing on the sunny side of their house. Mr. Náhlovský used to give us children grapes and sometimes even candy. We cried when the old man died. My mother was annoyed with us and grumbled, "You won't cry that much for me when I die!"

Maminka never ate the big red strawberries that grew on the hillside near our home. She was superstitious and believed that if she ate the berries, my dead brother, Pepa would be deprived of them in heaven. But her belief certainly did not stop us children from gorging ourselves on the fruit.

Considering how little meat we ate during those years, it's not surprising that I remember what I saw one day when my sister, Julča, and I were sitting on the footbridge over the creek. We were dangling our toes in the water when we noticed a big bug in the water. We ran excitedly to tell *maminka* who sent us to our neighbor, Najman. "That's not a bug, that's a crayfish," he told us. Najman pulled it out of the water and cooked it. I got a small piece, but I don't remember how it tasted—only that it was salty.

Another strange thing we ate during the war grew in the grassy area by our home. This is the area where we kept goats, but there were also some small low-growing thistles we called *pupavy*. They tasted milky and were a particular delicacy.

Finally, I remember our Christmas dinner that traditionally consisted of mushroom soup with barley, mushroom pie, and rolls with poppy seeds, butter and syrup. For dessert, we had nuts, apples, and dry apple pieces. Afterwards, *tatínek* played cards with us using nuts for money. With the neighbors, he played for matches. *Maminka* and *tatínek* tried to make Christmas a happy time with special treats, but our parents could afford so little. We never had a Christmas tree. We wouldn't even have known where to put it, our cottage was so small. We never received any gifts, but we looked forward to the dinner.

Chapter 2
Rovensko

Jára's background notes
Just prior to and during World War I: 1912-1918

Rovensko pod Troskami is the full name of the town, with the words *pod Troskami* indicating that it is near the site of an old castle ruin (Trosky), a place Mother talked about in chapter one. Today, Rovensko looks much the same as it did in the early 1900s. A small town in northern Bohemia, Rovensko now has a population of about 1,250.[3] When my mother lived there as a child, it had about a thousand more residents.[4] It is still located at least seven miles from even a small city, and it is still primarily a farming community with some light industry. Most of the buildings in town then still stand now. (Unfortunately, the cottage where Mother grew up is no longer there.) However, despite appearances, much has changed.

Czechoslovakia was part of the Austro-Hungarian Empire then. When the war broke out, men like my maternal grandfather were expected to fight for the ruling Hapsburgs, even though those conscripted often felt no loyalty or sense of belonging. They were peasants. Even though feudalism had ended in the Czech lands about fifty years earlier, the peasant class endured.[5] The concept of working class people with rights and freedoms did not begin to take hold until the 1920's, during the first Czechoslovak Republic. In contrast to today's car-centered society, peasants in small towns and villages stayed close to home. Mother describes how they looked forward to local celebrations, such as fairs and festivals, which sometimes commemorated an historical event and other times were merely an opportunity to relax and socialize. One such event was the annual witch-burning ceremony. Mother's letter speaks of burning a symbolic wooden stake, which was notably less barbaric than the medieval practice of igniting one's neighbors.

At the time when my mother was young, peasants in Bohemia often spent their lives in the village of their birth. Traveling long distances was difficult and impractical. As illustrated by my mother, walking and bicycling were the major modes of transportation. The train was also favored for necessary travel, like commuting to a job in Jablonec.

Mother and her neighbors in Rovensko could not travel for pleasure. In addition to their lack of money, they needed to work every day. With limited travel and few official sources of news, they had little knowledge of life outside their own community. Mother describes a small but intimate public, where most relevant news concerned the immediate surroundings. She also mentions buying a newspaper for a wealthier villager, and her story illustrates how special the newspaper was at that time. People occasionally exchanged letters, too, but word-of-mouth and gossip were the most available sources of news and entertainment. This news sharing often came from traveling peddlers, other train passengers, shopkeepers, teachers, and public officials.

When my mother was growing up in Bohemia, present-day concepts like self-awareness did not exist among the general population. Mother describes people who, it seems, were neither aware of alternatives nor driven by a desire to change. Her passages about the town's eccentrics show a great degree of toleration, although the line was drawn when it came to serious mental problems. The world Mother describes was one where odd people were tolerated, but those who were considered crazy (and would still probably be considered so) had no chance of receiving any beneficial treatment. The madhouse in Kosmonosy (a town in central Bohemia) was where "patients" were disposed of until they obligingly died. Without the niceties of the modern world, such as job retraining programs, counselors, and therapists, and with only meager medical care or legal recourse, the mildly mentally ill were largely on their own, the only help coming from whatever their families could provide.

For the merely disabled or elderly, Bohemians did have a safety net of sorts called *Domovské Právo,* which means "right of domicile." If a poor, homeless man were wandering the streets and a policeman picked him up, the officer could send him to the town of his father's birth. There he would be placed in a shelter with others like him. However, usually that's not what occurred. Generally, the immediate or extended family provided for needy relatives. Charities were virtually nonexistent, except for the church. But this institution was of limited assistance. Although the poor looked toward the church for charity, my mother always felt that most clergy were biased toward the wealthy, who could afford to give gifts and contributions to the church.

Mother's letter also discusses illness. This was a decade before Fleming discovered penicillin and long before the arrival of most pharmaceuticals as we know them today. The status of the science of the day meant that people with medical conditions could not expect much help from their doctors. To fill the void, people relied on friends and family for folk remedies, which frequently proved fatal.

A friend of mine told me the story of a small-town Czech doctor who used to eat dinner every Friday night in the home of an elderly woman and her two sisters, whom he had known practically all his life. After dinner, the lady would clear away the dishes, and the ritual would begin. With the four of them seated around the table, the doctor would reach for his black leather bag and put it next to him on the floor. Then each of the women, in turn, would recite her symptoms, aches and pains. After each was finished, the doctor would reach in his bag and pull out a little bottle of pills or liquid that he would ceremoniously hand to the speaker. Each of the women had relatives and friends who, although not present at the table, also had ailments that needed cures. Acting as proxy, the women would say something like, "Doctor, my Aunt Klára has been suffering from lower back pains. She sweats during the night and the bottom of her feet itch. What do you have for her?" The doctor would then reach into his trusty black bag and pull out a small bottle containing some mysterious ingredients that he would give to the speaker for her aunt. No money was exchanged. It was primarily a social evening among old friends. Instead of playing cards, they played the medicine game. Another way of looking at it is that presenting the hostesses with little bottles of hope was roughly equivalent to bringing a bouquet of flowers, a box of chocolates, or any other desirable treat. Many of these "medicines" contained high percentages of alcohol; others contained small but potent amounts of morphine, opium, cocaine, and even digitalis. Such cure-alls rarely cured anything, but they often made the sufferers feel better temporarily. The intent of the treatment as a palliative may have been understood by all (the same as we do today when we administer morphine).

Akin to these nostrums were various folk remedies. My mother, for example, believed that the steamy smoke belching from trains could help cure colds. She frequently took me and my brother to the railroad overpass when our heads were clogged so we could inhale the smoke. For the most part, people had to rely on such treatments that they could prepare and administer themselves.

Tiny amounts of arsenic have often been an ingredient in traditional remedies, so it's not too surprising that this was used in the Czech folk culture. (Coincidentally, in the United States, old advertisements, vintage 1880 from North Carolina and Virginia, sang the praises of a local bromine-arsenic springs. One of the claims was that the water would perk up the appetite and help those "low in flesh.")[6] Kerosine was also used in desperate situations, according to Mother. Many of these folk cures ended up killing the patient. But it seems likely that very sick patients would have died anyway; so the "cures" might have only sped up the process.

Included in Mother's letter describing her early life in Rovensko are several matter-of-fact references to deaths. According to a Czech proverb, "Where there is nothing, even death is nothing."[7] People died from almost every imaginable cause and often at early ages. So Mother's attitude is not particularly surprising; it only reflects the commonplace. The Czech population was kept low by a high infant mortality rate and virulent contagious diseases like tuberculosis, meningitis, and influenza. These illnesses were augmented by childbirth deaths, work-related accidents, a variety of mishaps in and out of the home, and suicides—as illustrated repeatedly in my mother's letters. Of course, death also resulted from the ravages of age, but only for those few survivors like Mother who managed to beat the odds along the way.

One thing I like about Mother's letters is that, in addition to describing the relentless hardships suffered by her and her equally poor neighbors, she also hints at the beauty of her natural surroundings. She lived in what is recognized today as one of the most picturesque parts of Bohemia. Her village of Rovensko, located in the center of this region, is known as Czech Paradise—a land of spruce forests, enchanting sandstone formations, and green rolling hills. Although life was difficult, many residents of Rovensko took advantage of these surroundings, including the many ruins of Gothic castles which still stand today.

Tonča's letter to Jára

I was nine years old when World War I broke out. As we usually did, I remember reading the latest posting on the town square bulletin board. I felt a cold chill as I read the dreaded "Proclamation of the Emperor" and "Declaration of Mobilization." Two weeks later, *tatínek* received his draft notice. Our family was devastated. We all cried and pleaded for Mayor Vrabec to help. He was a good man; he spoke up for us, probably writing to someone high up in the military who took care of hardship cases, and *tatínek* was released from military service. The mayor knew that our family was among the poorest in a village of poor families. If *tatínek* left for the military, who would care for his bedridden wife and house full of children?

It wasn't only *tatínek* who did his best to avoid the draft. Most village men realized that winning the war for the emperor would be of no particular benefit to them. They knew it would affect only wealthy merchants and those from the old nobility class. The emperor had no interest in improving the life of the simple poor. Whatever the outcome of the war, daily living in Rovensko would continue to be the same, and we all knew it.

Rovensko was a small town with a modest central district where the two major roads crossed. The town square was the civic center where buildings like the city hall, police station, post office, and several taverns, restaurants, and shops were located. In those days, people lived above their shops. The buildings were two and sometimes three stories high with the store or business on the ground floor level and the living quarters above. As you walked further away from the central area, the buildings gradually became one story homes. On the outskirts of town, they didn't really qualify as anything as grand as houses; they were small cottages like ours along the highway. A creek flowed directly in back of where we lived. The railroad tracks crossed over the creek and highway. In back of the highway and all around us were fields of crops, then hills, and further back, the forest.

Our cottage was divided into two side-by-side one-room apartments. Mr. Hrubý, his wife and family lived in the smaller apartment. He worked at home grinding garnets. She worked part time at the mill and tended the small family field where the family grew its vegetables. She did all the laundry, baked bread which she sold to the bakeries, and did odd jobs wherever needed. What's more, she often filled in as a midwife for cows and other animals. (Hrubá [Mrs. Hrubý] was the woman who revived me when I almost drowned in the creek when I was a little girl.) She was always very busy, but she did have a maid and teenage daughters who helped around the house.

Hrubý had a habit of snooping on us. Several times, I caught him with his ear pressed to the planks separating our apartments listening to what was going on in our place. He and his wife could see into our attic and we could see into theirs. Once during the winter, Hrubý was carrying two good-sized cans of water. He fell, pouring water all over himself. I saw what happened and burst out laughing.

The half of the cottage we lived in was a little larger because our one-room apartment also had a separate storage area. Inside, the apartment was dark. The only light that entered came from two small windows grouped together and another two windows on a connecting wall. The rough-cut pine furniture consisted of two long benches, a table, a bed, a single small chest of drawers, and a few kitchen shelves. This furniture was painted dark brown, which added to the dimness of the room. The floor wasn't like the ones we have today. Rather than a flat surface, the knotty pine boards made an uneven walking area, the bumpiness due to the contrast between the hard knots that kept their thickness and the wood around it that gradually disappeared through natural wear and frequent scrubbings. Fortunately, the smoke from our oven escaped through a pipe directly into our chimney. The only time our room filled with smoke was when *tatínek* and his friends took out their pipes and lit up.

Our neighbors in the next house, the Koženýs, didn't have any children, but that didn't stop me from going there to play. Once when I was visiting, Kožená pointed to a basket holding her sewing things and eyeglasses. "Don't touch the eyeglasses, then you won't break them," she warned. Of course, since she spoke so excitedly, I was attracted to them. When I took the glasses in my hands, the lenses immediately fell out of their frame. I thought, "Now I'm going to get it!"

The next day, I heard her calling me. Still frightened and certain that she would punish me, I approached cautiously. But instead of scolding, she said, "Go into town and buy me a lottery ticket." She gave me some money and didn't mention anything about the eyeglasses. I was very relieved. Perhaps she knew that the frame was loose and the lenses always fell out; in any case, she didn't make anything of the incident. But to be on the safe side, I didn't visit my godmother, Kožená again for a long time.

In the wheat fields

My guilt feelings didn't stop me from helping in the Kožený family's wheat fields nearby. The farm workers harvested the grain by hand, whacking away with scythes. It was the women's job to collect armfuls of wheat. In particular, my task was to collect the sheaves, bundle them up, and tie them together with pieces of straw. There they would stay in the field, each bouquet resting up against the other until they were dry and brittle. After several hours of work, I had enough. Kožená paid me what she could afford—some bread and butter and an armful of grain so big that I could barely manage to carry it home. I was happy that I could contribute something to the family.

We children also helped with gleaning. After the reaping was done, we were allowed to take home any straw or scatterings of grain left behind on the ground. We wanted the straw because it usually still had bits of grain clinging to it.

Other fields were less welcoming. My sister, Růža, and the Boum children, who lived close-by, once got into trouble playing in the fields that belonged to the local nobility. I remember seeing Růža running with the Boum children who had suddenly dashed off with a sheaf of wheat. The guard raced after them. I rushed over and soon we were all running as fast as we could. The Boums got away, but the guard caught Růža and me. He took our baskets and led us to the police station. We cried all the way over there. Fortunately, nothing serious came of the incident. The women working in the fields told the policemen that I was innocent and that Růža hadn't done anything wrong either.

The same couldn't be said of the Boum children. They were born thieves. The eight of them never hesitated to snatch anything that caught their eyes. They even stole a stick from our backyard that we used for hanging laundry. Once, they tried to steal our hens, but my sister, Máňa, chased them away. They also took the laundry drying on a clothesline outside the mill.

Their father, old man Boum, deserted from the Austro-Hungarian Army. There were many Czech deserters from that war; who would want to fight for the Kaiser? Boum escaped from the army camp when it was dark, late at night, and made good progress along the road by the time he was discovered missing the next morning. The military police telegraphed the local police in Rovensko, figuring that Boum was heading home, which is exactly what he did. What a foolish man!

The Rovensko police thought they were going to make a quick arrest. The policemen almost had Boum trapped in his cottage, but he made up in speed what he lacked in brains. He was able to escape through the trap door in his attic. He quickly climbed out onto the roof of their one-story cottage, looked around, and leaped to the ground on the side away from the searching eyes of the three policemen. He ran off into the forest before the policemen realized he got away. Boum hid there for a long time, depending on his children to bring him food. We kids frequently went into that same forest to pick blueberries, but we stopped going because of the frightening noises we heard. We didn't know then that it was Boum trying to scare us away.

The Sahulka family

In another house nearby lived the Sahulka family. They had five children: three daughters and two sons. The youngest was still in his crib when their father was killed in the war. Their son, Tomáš, was drafted toward the end of the war, but he didn't stay around long. At the first opportunity, he deserted. Two policemen came after him to take him back to his division. The neighborhood girls, including myself, ran after Tomáš. Sobbing hysterically, we begged the policemen to let him go. Tomáš had his own plan. He asked his two escorts for permission to go aside (you know what for). When they released him, he ran down the slope, and leaped over the creek. But as he landed on the other side, he banged into a tree and fell into the water with a bloody, bruised head. The police pulled him out and took him away. It was already near the end of the war, and Tomáš soon returned home unharmed. I don't think he ever had to serve at the front.

Tomáš' sister, Manka, was hard-working, but his sister, Božka, was a shameless, lazy girl. She would visit Hrubý, for no reason, when his wife wasn't at home. Manka and I once saw Hrubý feeding Božka dried plums and freely touching her breasts. I am sure Hrubý didn't like us being there.

My sister, Julča, was working in a factory at the time, earning enough to attend dance classes. There, she met a young man who started coming around to ask her out. He was a licensed miller, but Julča didn't care for him. Instead, Božka caught him for herself. They got married, rented a mill, and soon were very well off. In fact, they became rich during the war and later bought the mill that they had been renting.

Toníček Medků

Toníček Medků was special to the people of Rovensko. You wouldn't think so by the way he looked. He was very short, slightly larger than a midget, with a deformity that made him hunchbacked. He stayed the same for many years, never seeming to age. Despite his unattractive appearance, people liked him, maybe because he smiled at them. Unlike most people, he was always patient and took time to listen. No one knew how old Toníček was. He himself didn't know. He never went to school. He wasn't allowed to go since he was crippled. His mother used to worry about what would happen to him when she was gone. In fact, she did die young, and Toníček was left all alone.

He had a little room, really a shed. He stored all kinds of junk in it besides some coal and wood for fuel. The city gave him a little money, but not enough to live on. Toníček had no training or knowledge of the outside world. To bring in additional money, he made paper castles by cutting out shapes from cardboard boxes and pasting the pieces together. He sold these cardboard castles to the villagers.

Eventually, Toníček started a real business. He went to Lomnice to buy crackers and to Jičín for his sweet pastries. Toníček became a peddler. He sold needles, thread, shoelaces, prayer beads, pictures of the saints—I don't know what else. He walked from village to village selling his merchandise at fairs and carnivals. When there was a dance at the city hall, he had a little table there with his goods on display.

Later, Toníček bought a cottage with one big room and another slightly smaller, more like a shed. In his larger room, there was a wide window where he displayed all his goods. Everything was tidy. He cooked for himself, did the laundry, and cleaned the house. What impressed me most was a picture he had. Surprisingly, it was really a music box. He played it for me sometimes when I came to see him.

One of Toníček's friends put an ad in the paper to find Toníček a wife. A woman answered the ad and sent a photo of herself. When Toníček sent her back his own picture, that ended his romantic adventure. Nevertheless, he cherished her picture and bragged that she couldn't visit him because of the war. Later, he told people that she probably died in the war.

After awhile, Toníček sold the cottage with the condition that he could continue to live in one of the rooms for the rest of his life. That's where he eventually died in 1938. For several days, he lay on the floor before his neighbors found him. Many people came to his funeral. They say that some unknown good soul later dug up his ashes in the churchyard and buried them closer to the wall, a holier site.

The Doležal family

As it was every year at the end of April, there was a frenzy of activity to prepare for the witch-burning ceremony, and it really looked like it was going to be big that year (before the war, probably 1913). Men from our town of Rovensko on that special day were busy hauling wood, barrels of tar, and kerosine up the steep hill. They stacked the wood in a huge pile. After dusk, at the top of the hill, the men planned to light a large fire. In other nearby villages, much the same was happening. On the thirtieth of April, after sundown, we would see the fires burning on the hilltops all around us.

I watched the men prepare for the witch-burning. Later, back home, as I was entering our garden, I saw Jarka Doležal. He was running and looked panic stricken. He leaped over the creek and quickly disappeared into the shrubbery. Minutes later, I heard someone shouting, "It's burning. The stake is burning!" The people of Rovensko were angry and disappointed because Jarka started the fire ahead of the appointed time. Jarka didn't sleep at home that night because the men were watching his house. They didn't catch him right away, but I know they got him later and gave him a beating.

Jarka's mother was a crabby, sour-faced woman. She didn't talk to us or, for that matter, to anyone else; I don't know why. Since she was so unpleasant, we didn't allow her to pass through our property to reach the creek that she needed for bathing and laundry. Instead, she had to go two houses down the road and walk through the Lhotský's property. I remember once hearing shouting. I ran over to take a look. I saw Lhotský throw Doležalová's laundry into the water. Then he smacked her hard and shoved her into the water as well. My parents made me promise not to tell anyone. They didn't want me to be called as a witness and have to go to court. They firmly believed that nothing good could come out of getting involved with the law.

The Doležals' sons both attended the university in Praha [Prague]. I don't know how their parents were able to afford it; the family was very poor. They had only a small cottage, a goat, and a little land. How the Doležals made a living was a mystery. We suspected something shady. Were they stealing money from somewhere? In any case, they had their share of tragedy. The elder son went crazy when he was twenty-five and died in the madhouse in Kosmonosy. Jarka's father, who worked as a foreman at the flour mill, was killed when he fell against a fast-moving belt.

Malicious neighbors

Our neighbors, the Kudibál family, rented some rooms in their home to another family, the Štrnads. This family had a son, a hunchback with a mean, scheming nature. Just to be nasty, he made up lies about me. He claimed that I said the mill keeper's son, Vašík, had consumption and would die soon. I didn't say anything like that. Where would I get such an idea? Vašík heard these lies, so he and his brother, Láďa waited for me in ambush when I was delivering newspapers and beat me up. Strangely enough, Vašík really did die young, but not of consumption. By coincidence, I happened to be there when his funeral procession passed, moving from the mill to his family grave. I hung around for a few minutes then continued on my way.

The grave was in a nice spot in the cemetery close to our family plot where *maminka* and *tatínek* were eventually buried. Almost ten years after *tatínek's* death, my stepmother sold the family plot. The new owners dug up my parents' remains to prepare room for the burial of their family members in years to come. Since all cemetery contracts expired in ten years, the bones would have been removed soon anyway to make room for more dead bodies. (As you know, old bones are reburied in a pit in the corner of the cemetery, unless, of course, a family makes other arrangements.)

The Hájek family

During the first years of the war, my daily duty was to deliver the Praha newspaper to the Hájeks. For that I'd get a pastry or piece of bread and a cup of coffee plus fifteen *krejcar* [pennies] per month. Hájek and his wife were good people. Brožek, who owned a small shop in the village, used to wait for me to stop by on my way so he could read the newspaper too. He would give me a hard brightly-colored candy for my trouble. On Sundays, the foreman from the mill also used to wait for me to arrive with the paper.

The Hájeks once gave me a black smock with red trim. I wore it to school on picture-taking day.

During his working years, Hájek used to be a clerk with the railroad. Unfortunately, his pension during the war years became all but worthless because of inflation. In the later years of the war, out of money and things to barter, he had to move his family to a remote village where living was cheaper.

Bad advice

The Vošmrda family lived across the street. When the war started in 1914, Vošmrdová sent her husband to his death by insisting that he take a job digging trenches for the soldiers fighting on the front lines. At that time, the military was recruiting middle-aged men, too old to serve in the army, to dig trenches. The government encouraged men to sign up by promising to help their families. Vošmrda didn't want to go, but his wife drove him to accept the work by her constant nagging. It wasn't long before she heard that her husband was killed, caught in crossfire on the front lines—as were many men digging those trenches.

Later, I became reacquainted with their daughter, Monika. This was in 1925, Jára, when you were an infant. Monika had met a local man from Rovensko whom she fell madly in love with. But she didn't think she was pretty enough because she was skinny, so she decided to put on some weight. Taking her girlfriend's advise, she began swallowing small doses of arsenic on a daily basis. That helped her fill out, and she looked much better. After that, she made it part of her regular diet. She and her boyfriend got married and had twins who died at birth. Then she had a son, but she died when he was four. Monika had cut out the arsenic completely, all at once, and the shock to her system killed her. Why didn't her girlfriend warn her? She must have known that you have to taper off gradually from arsenic!

The sorrowful state of our everyday lives

On the other side of the street from us was a blacksmith shop where the smith, a muscular man, was always at work. He was a kind man who used to lend us a sled in the wintertime. His wife was frail, skinny and always sick. When she died, the blacksmith hanged himself.

Next to the smithy was a small house where three young unmarried sisters once lived. I used to see them every day when I was walking to school. Then, six months later, I didn't see any of them anymore. I wondered where they were. Then I heard they all died of consumption; their father, too. We had to get used to that.

Down the road from our house was the grain mill where my friend, Mařenka, and her parents lived and worked. The mill consisted of a simple machine: a primitive water wheel and grinding stones. Of the mill keepers' eight children, three of them died young. Mařenka became ill with meningitis when she was only eight years old and was gone in three days. That same year, the mill keepers' twenty-year-old son died. I saw him laid out in the coffin. After the others left, I stood there all alone, staring at him lying in the hall. You might think I'd have been spooked, but I wasn't. About seven years later, the mill keeper's wife drowned herself when she discovered that her husband kept a mistress. His lover was a young girl who worked at the mill.

On the other side of the grain mill was the saw mill. When it was sunny, we kids would run over to the sawmill and play on the pile of logs. It felt muggy and the heat was stifling, but we didn't mind. Over the years, though, the mill became less and less profitable and finally the owner had to close its doors.

When workmen were clearing out the saw mill, one of them discovered the body of a man buried in the sawdust. The rumor I heard was that he was one of the Italians who helped build the railroad. It was backbreaking work, and the Italians who worked there rarely had family nearby to come home to in the evening. They were never really a part of Czech society. Did the Italian worker die in an accident? Probably, when you consider how little safety protection he had as a laborer, and a foreign one at that.

We had three or four Italian refugee families camped out in nearby Ktová during the war. Every day they walked over to the mayor's house and lined up with the others to receive free soup. The dole was one bowl per person. I used to go there to get some, too. The bowlful was enough for me, but it wasn't enough to fill up those hungry Italians. They scavenged the hillsides collecting snails, snakes, even earthworms, and they ate them all.

Almost all the people of Rovensko and the surrounding area were Christian Czechs like us, with only a few exceptions. In addition to the Italian refugees and workers, I remember two Jewish families—probably because their young children, Klára and Rebeka, attended school with me. When Klára died, the mourners accompanied her body to the city boundary (close to where we lived, just behind the bridge) before they turned back, maybe to take the train to another town to bury her in a special cemetery for Jewish people. I felt sad about losing Klára. We had been friends.

Community happenings

In 1916, when the country celebrated the coronation of Emperor Karl I, government people handed out free sausages. Actually they piled them on the floor of the Rovensko city hall. After awhile the sausages began to smell awful. We ate them anyway and nothing happened to us. It was wartime and we ate everything. We didn't know about the dangers of food spoilage, but we probably wouldn't have worried if we had; we saw ourselves as hardy people.

The city hall, facing the large town square, was sometimes used as a theater. I remember one performance that no one expected. In those days, since there was no electricity, carbide gas was used for lighting. The gas was piped into our city hall from a big caldron that simmered outside in the town square. It was the responsibility of the policeman on duty to keep watch over the pot. Well, one of these policeman wasn't paying attention. He walked over to the caldron with a lit cigar. Wow, what an explosion! All the windows shattered in the square and the force of the blast extended out into the surrounding community. It shook our house and rattled the windows, but none were broken because our house didn't face the square. Later, the clean-up crew scraped off pieces of the policeman from all over the area.

Schooling during World War I

Rovensko had a one room schoolhouse where I learned how to read and write. But we also discovered hidden lessons outside our school books. My experience at school taught me that priests are obliging to the rich, but scornful of the poor.

I'm not against religion. Everyone has a right to believe as he wishes. But I haven't respected priests since my schooldays. My teacher, a priest, only liked pupils from rich families. They could afford to give him money and gifts. On the other hand, poor families were barely able to clothe their children. Most of the time, we went barefoot.

During wartime, when the priest received contributions of wooden shoes to distribute to the poor, he didn't want to give me any. (Once, my uncle came to see us and took me to town and bought me a pair of wooden shoes. During the war, we either went barefoot or wore wooden shoes. Only on Sundays did I wear a pair of leather shoes that *tatínek* had the cobbler make for me.) Even though the priest knew I attended church every Sunday, he challenged me with the same questions, "Do you attend church? Do you pray?" I always reported that I was with my *row*. Being with the row meant that we children assembled in the classroom, as we were seated, and walked to the church together that way.

Sometimes after a long dry-weather period, we children used to gather outside the schoolroom and, with a priest leading the way, hike together over to the fields where we found *mukas* and crosses. We stopped at those places and prayed for rain. The *mukas* were stone shrines six or seven feet tall. Near the top of each one was an opening that held a small statue of Jesus or a saint. I have seen other *mukas* in village courtyards made of stuccoed brick. No matter where they were, they served as religious altars, places of prayer.

I don't know who placed those *mukas* in the countryside. Some of them probably have been there for centuries. I heard that people put them where bad things happened, such as murders or terrible accidents. But I know some *mukas* were put there just because villagers needed a convenient place to pray while they were working in the fields. I myself never paid any attention to *mukas* except for the times during my schooldays when we went there to pray for heavy rains.

The priest's favorite student was Helena, the daughter of a successful businessman. The priest acted differently towards Helena than he did towards me. She once told him that I was a bad girl and that I smelled. He immediately ordered me to stand behind the door. In fact, it was Helena who stank. I had an empty stomach, but she was over fed. I never forget when someone accuses me of something unjustly, like when the Štrnad boy lied about me and I was beaten by the mill keeper's sons for things I never said.

Although we were much more innocent than kids are today, we did have our ways of annoying teachers. A favorite pastime in my religion class was teasing our catechism teacher. We were guilty of two common pranks: putting chalk marks on his coat and dirtying the edge of the bench that he leaned on while teaching us. That's pretty mild stuff today; however, in those days, such things were considered misbehaving.

School was different then. Teachers weren't allowed to marry, but that doesn't mean they never had affairs. In fact, I served as messenger for my favorite teacher who was deeply in love with the married director of our school. They counted on me to deliver notes from her to the director. These notes tucked inside a book told where the two lovers arranged to meet. She was emphatic that I give the book only to the director. Many times I saw her walking down the road to meet him on the path above the railroad tracks over by the meadow near the creek. In time, she became pregnant and had a daughter. My teacher's mother raised her granddaughter secretly in Praha, but I only learned that later. I liked that teacher and learned a lot from her in class.

On the other hand, I didn't learn too much from my fourth grade teacher, Miss Rušovská. She didn't know how to teach and had little interest in helping the poor children learn. In spite of her, I passed all of my subjects except division. That was because we started studying division a few days before I left school on April 23, 1919. I have found that during my whole life not knowing division has never been a problem.

City improvements

The first train from Turnov to Jičín started service in 1903. The tracks passed by our house on the other side of the creek. Electricity and street lighting came to Rovensko when I was about twelve years old, but our family and many others in town weren't hooked up. It was expensive, and we didn't have the money. Of course, we were all still excited about the light from the small bulb on the street; we thought it was wonderful. One of the light poles was near our house and *maminka* wanted to see it. By this time, in 1917, *maminka's* condition made her unable to walk. *Tatínek* carried her in his arms to a spot where she could see the new street lighting.

Chapter 3
On My Own

Jára's background notes
First Republic: 1918-1921

Mother tells us that in Rovensko, the end of World War I was cause for great celebration. It was also the beginning of a new nation in Czechoslovakia—our First Republic under President Tomáš G. Masaryk. This new independent Czechoslovak Republic included over thirteen million people.[8] Besides Czechs and Slavs, there were Germans, Hungarians, Ukrainians, Ruthenes, Poles, Russians, Jews and a small number of other ethnic minorities such as Rumanians and "gypsies," all within our national boundaries.[9] Masaryk began his presidential term acting on his promise to make Czechoslovakia a nation founded on morality and social justice.[10] He launched many progressive changes such as school reforms, land redistribution, unemployment benefits and an eight hour work day.[11] Yet, notwithstanding these national reforms, local government experienced little change in the villages and small towns like Rovensko. Before 1918, the governing body was composed of the chairman of the parish council, the parish priest, and the head teacher of the local school. Later, depending on the size of the village or town, it was governed by a mayor and, perhaps, a small city council, as was the case in Rovensko.[12]

Writing about her experiences during this time, Mother mentions the role of the church. The Catholic Church and Protestant denominations have had their ups and downs in Czechoslovakia. The country has had a history of Protestantism since the days of Jan Hus, who Mother discusses. Hus was a priest and reformer who founded the first reformed church in all of Europe, one hundred years before Martin Luther.[13] Hus was burned at the stake in 1415 for his unorthodox views. From long before my mother's time, and up to today, Jan Hus is remembered and revered by Czechs.

Nevertheless, the Catholic Church has historically played a dominant role in Czech religious life. Under the rule of Emperor Ferdinand II (1619-37), non-Catholic priests were banished from Bohemia. Protestant nobles and burghers were forced to choose between conversion or banishment and Catholicism was declared as the sole permitted religion.[14] At the end of World War I, when Czechs were finally freed from the Hapsburg regime, many Catholics bolted from the Church, in large part because they were angry at the Church for supporting the hated Hapsburgs.[15] New churches, such as the Evangelical Church of the Bohemian Brethren, were started in the post-WWI era.[16] For the first time in modern history, Czechs and Slovaks were free to worship as they wished.

From what I saw, most parishioners who remained in the Catholic Church did so on a secular basis. They considered themselves Catholic, but did not attend church or believe in the church's teachings any more. When they celebrated Catholic holidays, it was done more as a cultural expression than as a religious observance. With all the political shenanigans within the Church through the centuries, many Czechs developed a skeptical attitude toward religion. This skepticism intensified and eventually became atheism during the years of suffering at the hands of a series of regimes, especially the Communists (who strongly discouraged religion), and it still persists.[17]

This rejection of religion perhaps contributed to what comes through in Mother's letters as a cultural tolerance toward suicide in Bohemia. In my four-member immediate family alone, three people including my mother either attempted or succeeded in committing suicide. My mother relates tales of what seem like endless numbers of people trying their hand at suicide. In addition to the fact that many Czechs were not deterred by religious considerations, I suppose that a high incidence of dejection, hopelessness, and alcoholism contributed to the problem.[18] In Bohemia, there seemed to be no law or strong cultural prohibition against suicide. Also, people were undoubtedly desensitized to death in general because illnesses and accidents took so many lives. Suicide was just one more cause of death. In *Disturbing the Peace*, Václav Havel wrote (in 1986, three years before the beginning of his presidency) that he not only respects suicides for the courage it takes to commit the act but also, in a certain sense, because it places the worth of life very high. His reasoning was that it might devalue life to continue a pointless existence without love, hope, or meaning. Havel muses, "Sometimes I wonder if suicides aren't in fact sad guardians of the meaning of life."[19]

My mother's suicide attempts showed that she faced struggles that at times seemed insurmountable. As she writes, a major part of these struggles involved finding decent work. For most of her life, she worked for a series of farmers and small business owners. Some were quite well off, but others were barely able to feed their own families. No matter what their economic standing, they were generally able to hire a maid like my mother; wages for household help, farm workers, or any other kind of unskilled labor amounted to a shockingly trivial amount.

In her earlier letter, my mother mentioned that most of the residents of Rovensko did not usually travel far from home. However, she frequently walked or rode her bike to the neighboring small towns. Typical of her destinations were Ktová, Újezd, and Libuň, one to four miles from Rovensko, where she might go to attend a fair or local dance. For shopping, she went to Turnov, the nearest city, about seven miles away.

The young men my mother met came from these neighboring towns or farms. Usually a girl met a boy through introductions, at church, or at fairs or dances. As Mother discusses in the following letter, social life and dating were necessarily limited in scope. The people in Rovensko could not afford anything more extravagant.

Tonča's letter to Jára

World War I ended for us the twenty-eighth of October, 1918. On that day, we children wore the tricolor of the Czech flag—red, blue, and white—on our clothing. We celebrated the beginning of a new nation, Czechoslovakia. Cheering men and women rode through Rovensko in their horse-driven carriages carrying miniature gallows. They forced those who we all knew had profited from the war to kiss the hangman's noose.

A month later, the fourteenth of November

Maminka had suffered for thirteen years ever since her fall and miscarriage. Every year she got weaker and weaker. She just wasted away. I was with *maminka* when she died. *Tatínek* was also by her side. Růža was there too, but she had the Spanish flu and was nearly delirious from a high fever, barely aware of what was going on. Julča was at work; she had the graveyard shift at the jam and jelly factory. "Don't cry. Don't make my leaving difficult," were *maminka's* last words. And then she died. Even though it was three o'clock in the morning, my father sent me out to bring Anča back from the home where she worked as a maid. Heartbroken, I picked my way over dark fields and through four villages to Podůlše. There wasn't a single light in any of the farmhouses. It was dawn as Anča and I walked through our front door.

Those days when *maminka* was ill are gone, and I wouldn't want them back for anything. But I do have one sweet memory of that time. My sister, Máňa, gave me a little notebook for Christmas. I have it here in front of me. I remember how happy I was to receive it. Looking at the book, I see messages from my mother, father, sisters, two teachers and some schoolmates. One teacher I liked very much wrote this verse:

The misfortune of a nation is its poverty
The misfortune of a spirit is its ignorance
The misfortune of a heart is its hatred.
                    Written 2, March 1919

Where are all those people today? No longer alive. Every note and comment in my notebook is a memory. I am looking at the handwritten notes of three schoolmates who ended their lives by committing suicide. I also have a mountain lily pressed in my book from my school years. It is dry, but still holding up.

Suicidal wishes

Maminka frequently talked about committing suicide. I remember her saying to me when she was in pain, "If I could get out of this bed, I would go drown myself." I inherited my suicidal wish from her. In fact, the first thoughts I had about my own death came to me the day she died. I was herding goats in a place where a tall berry bush grew that people said was poisonous. With *maminka* gone, I felt like tempting fate. I ate some berries, but only got a stomachache.

The second time I tried to end my life was when I was collecting wood with Julča in a little forest near our house. I tried to carry a huge pile of wood hoping that the strain would kill me. This may seem like a strange way for a woman to kill herself, but that's what I was trying to do. Years later, I attempted suicide again; this time I was much more determined. That was when I was in Jablonec working as a maid. The lady I worked for scolded me for something; I don't remember what, but it made me feel sorry for myself. During the night, I gradually let the gas escape from the jet on the stove so it wouldn't make any noise. I was afraid that the lady would come in the kitchen and discover what I did. Close to morning, when I was nearly dead, I crawled to the balcony and opened the door. It was winter, and the fresh air quickly brought me back to life.

My stepmother and her sons

A year and a half after *maminka*'s death, *tatínek* remarried. Oddly, I first heard about the marriage from the church banns announcing his intention to marry the widow, Pospíšilová. She had three sons. My stepbrothers, Jarda, Růda, and Josef, were friendly, well-built, good-natured fellows. Jarda and Josef were about my age. They studied black smithing, apprenticing under a master blacksmith. But neither of them ever actually practiced their trade. Instead, Jarda got a job driving a bus and Josef worked for the state railroad system in Turnov.

Jarda asked me to marry him, but I didn't want to. He wanted children and I didn't, at least not then and not with him. After some time, he married someone else. Years later, he and his wife had a son. The son drowned when he was twenty. Jarda died relatively young, at about age sixty.

Růda, who became a tailor, practiced his trade only in winter. In summer, he worked in the fields. He died when he was only forty. He keeled over while eating some sweets at a wake in Rovensko.

Working on the farms (1919-1922)

Five months after *maminka's* death, on my fourteenth birthday (April 23, 1919), I finished my schooling and moved to Lažany. I found a job working for a farmer's family. I will tell you about one day that stands out in my memory. On this day, the farmer's wife and I set out for Turnov, with me carrying a big basket on my back. The basket contained a large goose to deliver to the home of a government official. We stopped at the main square in Turnov to drop off the goose and then walked over to Souček's hard liquor brewery. The farmer's wife purchased a large decanter of brandy, which I lugged back to the farm in a canvas knapsack. That was the first time in my life I drank a cumin brandy.

The farmhouse was a good place to work. My only problem was with the older boy in the family. I didn't like him because he always wanted to fight with me. He was about thirteen, well fed and strong. Once he threw me into a puddle of water. I was small and weak from the poor nourishment of a wartime diet. I guess that's why I appreciated the good food at that house so much. I can even remember it today. Unfortunately, I was there only until Christmas. At that time, the farmer's wife told me to go, that I wasn't needed any more. I never knew why.

My next job I called "the devil's service." From ages fifteen to seventeen, I toiled for sixty crowns per month for the Mazánek family, keeping myself alive on a miserable diet. To give you an idea of how much sixty crowns were worth at that time, a pair of ordinary shoes cost about two hundred and fifty crowns. Working in Václaví for this family was the worst job I ever had. I served them as a farm hand in the fields and as a maid in their large farmhouse.

My first day of work began in the month of January. It was cold and rainy. Every day, I worked in the fields until dark, along with the other servant girls. Below the farmhouse was a small creek where we washed off the mud-covered beets we had just uprooted. After an exhausting day outside, we were then required to clean out the stable.

At night, we girls slept in the farmhouse high up in the loft. Our bed was under the skylight, which let the snow fall on our beds and comforters. Each of us had one thin blanket, which gave us little protection from the freezing nights. Even though my shivering kept me awake, it never occurred to me to ask for another blanket. We slept two to a bed, snuggling together to keep warm. The bed was short; we couldn't even stretch out. I remember that once I fell off the bed, but I continued to sleep until the cold woke me up.

Every night, we left our shoes behind under the staircase and ran upstairs to bed barefoot because we weren't allowed to wear shoes upstairs. The farmer's wife was afraid we might track dirt from the fields onto the stairs. In the morning, we did the reverse, running down the stairs to put those very cold shoes on again. I used to suffer so much from cold feet. I was only lightly dressed because I didn't have any warm clothing. I wonder now why I don't have rheumatism today.

Sick and hurt

Once when I was working at the Mazánek's, I had a terrible sore throat. I wasn't able to swallow, but I had to take the cows to pasture anyway. I was standing next to the road when my stepmother's father walked by. I ran to him and gestured, not able to talk. Understanding my problem, he advised, "Put a cold, wet cloth on your neck with a dry one over it." I did what he recommended and a miracle happened: the swelling went down. By the morning, I felt fine again.

Another time, I was spreading straw behind the barn with an older servant when I noticed some unripe apples growing nearby. Although I knew they weren't ready to pick, I was very hungry and ate them anyway. In the evening, there was a dance at Tatobity that I went to with my girlfriend. I had just entered the room when a girl, someone I didn't know, approached me and offered me an apple. I ate it and immediately became violently ill. I guess that last apple was one too many. I ran outside and over to the cemetery next door where I began heaving. For a long time, I remained there leaning against the cemetery wall. At any other time I would have been too scared to stay, but at this time I was too sick to care. How I got home I don't remember. I spent the rest of the night in the outhouse with my head bent over the hole. In the morning, I was so exhausted that I could barely stand on my feet.

Mazánková didn't care enough to send me to bed, but realizing how weak I was, gave me an easy job that wouldn't tax my energy. She said, "Go to the field and see if you can find the tether chain that one of the workers left there." I walked just a short distance, then I stopped, unable to take another step. I collapsed on the ground. I either fainted or fell asleep, but when I woke up, I felt better. I even was able to find the lost horse chain.

I also remember walking behind two horses turning a grinding wheel pulling on a pole. Suddenly, I felt a blow to my knee that threw me to the ground. The horses stopped moving and a worker ran over to help me to my feet. My knee throbbed with pain. I knew immediately that it was farmer Mazánek's fault that I got hit with the pole. The horses should have been attached to the pole by a strong rope, but the rope frayed and the stingy farmer replaced it with a flimsy wire. When the wire broke, the pole swung back and hit me.

My companions sent me to find the doctor in Rovensko, which would normally be about a half-hour walk away. That day, with my painful knee, it took me two hours to cover the distance. I had to rest at every milestone marker. When I finally reached the doctor's office, he hollered at me, "Where is your insurance ticket?" How could I have picked up the ticket from the insurance company in Turnov, about three hours walk from where I had the accident, and then walked two hours more to the doctor's office? But that was the way the system was set up at that time. The doctor didn't get paid without an insurance ticket. So although I was hurting badly, the doctor expected me to make a special trip to the insurance office before going to him for treatment.

Flinching from the doctor's glare, I began to cry from pain and fright. Finally, he gave me a bandage with medication for my knee. I limped out of his office and somehow managed to walk to my parents' house. I stayed there and rested for two days. I was lucky that my knee wasn't broken or shattered.

Festival in Václaví

I remember a festival in Václaví that took place on top of a big hill. During the holiday of *Jan Hus,* the villagers made a torch by igniting a big wooden stake. Then they gathered together in a group to sing *Hranice vzplála* ["It started to ignite, the fire went up"]. I remember standing outside the Mazánek's farmhouse listening to the people sing and I joined in and sang along with them. My employer, Mazánková, came running out of the house and ordered me to stop singing. Her brother, who was a Catholic priest, was visiting. He didn't want anyone associated with his family to take part in the celebration honoring Jan Hus.

When *maminka* was little, she used to sing in a choir and help in the rectory. She was a devout Catholic, but I never took after her. I did attend church at various times throughout my life, but the last time I went to confession was when I was fifteen. I remember, it was during my first year working as a maid at the farmhouse. Mazánková sent Madla (another maid) and me to confession. The priest asked me, "Are you having intercourse?"

I responded, "I don't know what that means."

Then he asked me, "Do you have a boyfriend?"

"No," I answered. He sent me to the altar anyway to say three Hail Marys.

The servants at the Mazánek's farm were harvesting clover when another fair came, this time to Tatobity. We wanted to go, but weren't allowed to. Although the farmer's wife was very religious, she forced us to work most Sundays. Now I wonder why we didn't say anything. Maybe we instinctively knew if we did, we would end up like our work leader. He protested about the conditions, so the farmer fired him. But Mazánek paid a price for his harsh treatment; he couldn't find anyone to replace his lead man. Mazánek had to persuade his own nephew to come and help out temporarily. In fact, the workers at the Mazánek farm rarely stayed long.

Of all the servants who worked there when I arrived, only Madla remained. Madla stayed because of a fellow she liked in the village. I stayed because I was stupid. Eventually, I left and Madla got married. We left behind two other servant girls, but they left soon after—in the middle of harvest time. They also didn't want to work all day in the fields, even on Sundays while other young people walked by on their way to the fair.

My journey with the Mazáneks' cow

It was a hot day in June. We were cultivating beets when a messenger came to tell me to return to the farmhouse. Mazánková's brother was waiting for me to go with him to bring a young cow to the village of Knížnice. Although it may not make sense to you, I got dressed up in my party clothes. I knew we would be passing through many villages and I wanted to look my best in case I should meet a good-looking fellow along the way.

It was about eleven o'clock in the morning when Mazánková's brother and I, leading the cow, started our journey on foot. We walked to Rovensko and then at the railroad station, followed the tracks to Lhotka. At about two o'clock, a storm blew in. The cow, which had never been out of the barn before, wasn't used to walking. With the storm adding to her distress, she balked even more. I had to push her along with a stick. The farmer's brother-in-law decided to stay in Lhotka to get out of the storm. But he ordered me to go on ahead. He warned, "Don't let the cow lie down because if you do, she'll never get up again."

The storm got worse, with strong winds, rain, and lightening. There I was alone in the fields with the cow. I was wet through to the skin, half expecting one of the lightening bolts to kill me.

Finally we made it to the village of Čimyšle where my sister, Anča, used to work as a maid. Pushing the cow along, I headed straight to the house at the end of the village. Fortunately, they remembered me from the days when I sometimes came to see my sister. They put the cow into the barn and gave her some grass to eat. I was as hungry as she was, but no one gave *me* any food.

When the rain stopped, the cow and I continued our journey through Libuň and then on to Kněžnice. Back then, there were no cars on the road. If there were, I wouldn't have been able to hold on to the cow. We arrived in Kněžnice at evening time. I hadn't eaten all day, so I was extremely hungry. But when I got to the farm, I saw the farmer's wife shoveling and aerating manure for fertilizer. I went over to help her because I knew they had no servants. They couldn't hold on to any help because of the way they treated their workers. Soon the farmer came over and put the harness on the horses while his wife and I went to get them feed. I was so tired and hungry I could barely move. When we finished with the horses, we were done for the day. The farmer's wife brought me in the house and gave me some tasteless oat porridge that was left over from lunch. That porridge was awful; I almost threw it up. I stayed the night, but I couldn't sleep at all.

Later that year, in November, the same farmer and his wife traveled from Kněžnice to Václaví to attend some local festivals. While in Václaví, they stopped in to see me where I was still working at the Mazánek place. The farmer walked over to me and slipped ten crowns into my pocket and said, "This is an advanced payment for January when I want you to start working for me." I didn't stop or answer. Instead, I continued on my way to the barn to pick up horse feed. As I worked, I thought about that cold, tasteless porridge the farmer's wife gave me the last time I was in their home.

Before the visitors left, I marched back to the Mazánek house and told the Kněžnice farmer, "I won't work for you."

He angrily answered, "You've already accepted the down payment." But I didn't cave in. Instead I threw the ten crown bill on the desk and ran out of the room.

Two sides of the coin

Farmer Mazánek and his wife had no children. I wondered why they were so stingy. Mazánková kept the bread locked up and doled it out like Christmas candy. She never put out butter or lard to spread on the bread, only sour cottage cheese mixed with skim milk. On Sundays, we always ate the same lunch: bread with horseradish sauce and very tiny pieces of smoked meat. We never had any soup. In winter, we servants were given pieces of pressed fried bacon that were so dry that they never stuck to the bread. The Mazáneks were misers. Of course, twenty-six years later in 1948, the Communist regime took over, and the Mazáneks' farm became part of a collective. Their stinginess did them no good in the long run because all their gains came to nothing when they lost the farm.

As strange as it may seem, when I think about my life, sometimes I think my happiest years were those two years I spent with the Mazáneks in Václaví, despite all the hardships. I have never felt as free or as joyous since then. (Jára, thank God that you haven't inherited my melancholy character. I'm glad that you are well off and happy in this world.) Back then, I was young, healthy, and cheerful. I sang from early morning on. The farmer's wife liked me and wanted to keep me happy enough so I'd stay with them.

For example, Mazánková allowed me to go on a pilgrimage to the top of Mt. Tábor near Lomnice. Our processional started in Rovensko, and all the way we sang religious songs. A priest was at the head of the group followed by his assistant, who led our singing. At Mt. Tábor, I bought a picture of St. Anthony, my patron saint. (I don't know what happened to it, but it disappeared at sometime in my life.) After the pilgrimage ended, I made it back to the farm on foot, although others took the train. Another nice thing the farmer's wife did was give me fabric so I could have a dress and coat made for myself. In 1920, it cost me three hundred crowns to have the tailor make me those outfits. More than three months' pay.

New clothes

It wasn't only Mazánková who noticed that I needed new clothes. My parents also saw that I didn't have anything decent to wear, so they bought me cotton fabric for a blouse and a skirt. I brought the fabric to the tailor and had him make me a two-piece outfit: a gray skirt and a white blouse with long sleeves. Mother and father also bought me gunnysack cloth for another dress. It was just after the war, and this was the cheapest fabric available. I had a dress made from it, but I hated to wear it because the material was rough—it scratched me terribly.

I remember one Sunday when *tatínek* waited for me after church to take me shopping. "I am going to take you somewhere to buy you something," he said. The shops were open on Sunday mornings then. We walked into a shop and he said, "Pick out what you want." I chose a red skirt for work. I wore it for the first time the day I returned to my job at the Mazánek farm.

On another occasion when I needed fabric for a dress, my parents took me to Turnov in a horse-drawn carriage. This time, I bought blue and white striped material. I still have a photograph of me wearing the dress made from that fabric.

One piece of clothing I never had when I was a young woman was a bra, which was too bad because I used to have big, firm breasts. My sister, Julča, envied me, particularly when we went together to the spa. She bought some ointment she saw advertised in the paper hoping it would increase the size of her breasts, but it proved useless.

The widower with only a mother

In Rovensko there lived a widower with a small farm. His nephew used to see me at church on Sundays and he would say, "You ought to marry my uncle, the farmer." When I laughed, he added, "Did you know he has a horse?" He neglected to tell me that his uncle also had two children.

There was another young man who came all the way from Libuň to tell my father that he wanted to marry me. In asking my father for permission, the farmer proudly confided, "I have a house and only a mother to care for." I remembered that farmer from the time we met at a fair in Újezd. He danced all the dances with me until the middle of the evening when he bent over and whispered, "I have to go home now and feed my cows, but I'll come back. Wait for me here." I didn't. Why would I wait for such a fool who would leave me waiting for who knows how long? I left quickly so that I would be home before dark.

At the time the farmer came to see my father, I was living and working in Václaví. Since my father had no particular objection to the young man, he sent him over to the Mazánek farm to see me. But I didn't pay any attention to the fellow. He just sat on the porch and watched me while I did my chores, bringing hay to the animals. When I showed no interest in him, he finally left and never tried to see me again.

Franta Landa: the fellow who chased after me

After my job was over in Václaví, I returned home to my family where I stayed two weeks, waiting for my sister, Máňa, to come by and take me to Jablonec with her. During that time, Franta, a local guy, invited me to a dance. He owned a nice brick house, but for some reason, he didn't have enough money or was unwilling to pay the admission price to the dance. Instead of coming in with me, he stayed out on the balcony, watching me as I danced with various fellows. Sometimes I danced with three different men during one dance number. He was jealous, although I don't know why. We had no relationship. I didn't have any romantic interest in him. In spite of that, he waited for me and we walked back home together. On another occasion, we went to a dance together in Lhota. But we weren't alone. His buddy came with us, which was fine with me.

Even though we never really started a relationship, Franta didn't stop pursuing me. I remember him appearing with a friend on the doorstep of the home in Jablonec where I worked after I left Václaví. I was surprised because Franta and I hadn't been writing to each other. A week later, a letter arrived from his buddy, who was working as a clerk in Turnov. He wanted to correspond, but I never replied. Later, when I was in Rovensko on vacation, Franta was there again, chasing after me. He asked me to walk with him in the evening, but I refused. I didn't feel anything for him; he was just a friend from childhood. The next year, when I was working at the Nováks, he came to say goodbye. He was leaving for his stint in the military and was in a big hurry because he had to catch a train. I was in the cellar at the time so we didn't even see each other. As far as I was concerned, all the better.

Franta didn't have my address at the place where I was living during the war. Also, by the time he returned from military service, I was already married. One day, your father and I rode two on a bike to attend a Sunday afternoon dance at Ktová near Rovensko. Franta happened to be there too. He came over to me and asked me to dance. He was really upset because I hadn't waited for him to finish his military service and marry him. The next day, when your father and I were returning to Turnov on our bicycle, the train passed by and Franta waved to us from the window. That really annoyed your father.

Franta eventually married and had two sons. I talked to him once again many years later. Now he is long dead.

Pavel Koubek

At eighteen years old, I wasn't thinking of marriage yet, but I had a lot of admirers—some that I didn't even suspect. One of these was Pavel Koubek. The Koubeks, my old neighbors in Václaví, had six children, two sons and four daughters. All of them were attractive, especially Aninka, who everyone said was a beauty. She was a slender, delicate girl with black hair and blue eyes. She never did strenuous work; her tasks were to string beads and embroider. Karla, one of the other daughters, was still in school. There was also sixteen-year-old Standa and her brother, Slávek, who had already left home and was making a living as a tailor. But not all went well for the Koubeks. Their married daughter, Mařenka, suffered complications during childbirth and died. And then there was their son, Pavel, the one I want to tell you about.

Pavel was handsome, but moody. He lived at home then and dated a girl from the neighboring village. He ran after her every evening and cursed her every morning. In the end, he married her when she became pregnant. Pavel also liked me, but I didn't pay any attention to him. I had no idea that he was interested in me. I used to talk to him when I visited his family just as I did everyone else. To make a long story short, when he got married, the bride's family hosted a wedding celebration in a nearby pub. Our family was invited, so I was there, too. Pavel came over to me many times to ask me to dance and offer me drinks. He paid more attention to me than to his bride. Of course, she was annoyed with him.

Years later, when I was over in Jablonec, I heard that his wife and child died from suffocation due to a clogged chimney. He was suspected of murder, but they couldn't prove anything. After some time, he killed himself in the same way, probably because of a bad conscience. Once, when passing through the cemetery in Rovensko, I saw a gravestone with his name on it. Not long after, I met his sister-in-law and I mentioned that I used to know Pavel. "He was a murderer," she muttered. When I visited the cemetery at a later date, the gravestone was gone. Maybe his family removed the marker, figuring it was better not to remember him.

Chapter 4
Jablonec

Mother lived much of her life in the towns of Rovensko and Jablonec. As she already explained, Rovensko was a very small town. On the other hand, Jablonec was a real city, larger than average, which had its legends as well as history. According to legend, nothing but an apple tree was left standing on the banks of the Nisa River after Catholic troops invaded and captured the city in 1469 during the Hussite Wars. The village was rebuilt seventy years later. *Jabloň* is the Czech word for apple tree, so the rough translation of the full name of the city, *Jablonec nad Nisou,* is "Apple Tree on the Nisa."[20]

The city of Jablonec is situated in a beautiful woodsy low mountainous area, but the weather is bitter cold in winter. Today, the countryside attracts skiers. But to my mother, it was the place where she labored to make a few crowns, enough to afford some warm clothing to withstand the harsh winters.

Mother's letter describes her work as a maid in Jablonec. Small-town people like my mother flocked to the city to find jobs with better pay than they could earn doing farm labor, home industry, or small factory work near their village homes. In cities like Jablonec along the German border, people found work in the jewelry and glass industries.[21] A single person didn't have it too bad, but life was difficult for people who were married and struggling to support a family. Mother told me that many of these young couples lived in poverty and suffered from exhaustion and poor health.

Another name associated with this city is Gablonz, the German name for Jablonec. When my mother lived there, many of the streets also had German names, such as *Gutenbergstrasse*. The German inhabitants often did not speak much Czech. In fact, German was the language of culture and the educated class in Bohemian cities throughout much of modern history.[22] It was not until the later part of the nineteenth century that Czech literature began to flourish and not until the end of that century that spoken Czech became the formal language of Czech society.[23]

The strong German presence in Jablonec that my mother writes about had its origin dating back to the latter part of the eighteenth century when Hapsburg Emperor Joseph II passed the Toleration Patent of 1781. This reform encouraged ethnic Germans to settle in Czech lands close to the German border. Joseph II, with his decree, removed much of the civil discrimination that existed for one hundred and sixty years against Protestants and improved the status of the Jews, in particular regarding land and business ownership.[24] Many of these ethnic German settlers were Jewish. (Remember, the German nation didn't exist until 1871.[25]) However absurd it may seem now, in hindsight, these German-speaking Jewish immigrants became victims of the Czechs' mounting bad feelings toward the dominance of German culture and influence. Later, this attitude developed into a full-blown anti-Semitism that pervaded Czech society. Unflattering stereotypes of Jews were common in Jablonec and, in fact, all of Bohemia and Moravia. This prejudice was reflected in my mother's casual comment about her employer, Jakub Janovský, a Polish Jew.

From the mid-1800s to the mid-1900s, anti-Semitism had a respected position in Czech society. This phenomenon was not restricted to physical stereotypes, such as *the Jewish nose*. Anti-Semitism was overtly expressed by renowned members of the literary community. Czech Jews were depicted as foreigners by writers as esteemed as Jan Neruda. They were caught in the middle between Czechs from the small towns, who viewed them with suspicion, and the Germans of the Austro-Hungarian Empire, who hated Jews as much as (or more than) they did Slavs.[26]

Tonča's letter to Jára

The weather in January, 1922 was freezing when Máňa and I took the train to Jablonec. I was almost seventeen and in need of a decent job. I hoped Máňa could help me find work as a maid in the home of some wealthy family. Her boyfriend, Konůpek (they weren't married yet), picked us up at Turnov. I had only summer clothing and a scarf that Mazánková had given me. Nothing I had was suitable for real winter weather. It was terribly cold in the streetcar riding from Rychnov to Jablonec, and the chill left me with a severe tonsil infection.

Máňa brought me over to an enormous villa, where she served as a maid. She hadn't told her employer that she was bringing me along. It was Máňa's plan to hide me in the villa for a few days. She didn't want the lady of the house to know I was there, especially now that I was sick. It was my good fortune that her mother-in-law lived upstairs. She was a very kind person and could speak Czech, unlike most everyone else in the area. I stayed with my sister for a couple of days while she and the mother-in-law nursed me through the worst of my illness. Máňa bought me warm underwear and Konůpek made me shoes. I had to pay them back in installments, but I was grateful for their help. With these clothes, I was adequately dressed for the cold winter weather.

Máňa's employer was a Czech woman, not German like most residents of Jablonec. She originally came from Robousy and settled in Jičín. Later, she moved to Jablonec and married a German husband. At first, they were quite poor, but they started a successful costume jewelry business and became well off. They bought a villa and built a workshop right next to it.

After I got married, I worked at that same villa at a drilling machine making jewelry. I earned up to 280 crowns per week, and that was very good money then. (At that time, you were a baby, Jára, and lived with the Vondras. Your father and I couldn't afford an apartment where we could live together as a family.)

Looking for work in Jablonec

For a very short time, I worked for a German family in a big house in Jablonec. It was already dark when I arrived at my first day of work on a cold January evening. I immediately pitched in, washing the dirty dinner dishes that had accumulated in the sink. I knew that where there's a big house there's bound to be lots of work, and I was right. I was happy because madam could speak to me in Czech.

Madam showed me where I would sleep. It was a small room, but warm. It was heaven compared to the cold attic at the Mazánek farmhouse in Václaví. At breakfast, soon after I arrived, one of the family's two boys asked me for a *Löffel*. I didn't understand what he wanted, so he got it himself. That's how I learned that *Löffel* meant spoon in German. Later that morning, somebody knocked on the door. I opened it to find a German maid reporting for service. Madam had hired her and told me to go.

Desperate for a job, I asked Máňa to accompany me while I went door-to-door looking for work. One of the people we talked to told us of a possible job opening, so we went to the apartment house and started climbing the stairs. On the way up, we came upon Fanča, a childhood friend of mine. She was struggling to push a baby stroller up to the fifth-floor landing. When she heard why we were there, she said, "You wouldn't want to work for that family. I was glad to get rid of that job. You have to take care of their child and carry coal up the stairs. There's no elevator. And you have to do all the cleaning."

"Is that so?" I responded. "I heard they were a young couple and often have chicken to eat at their table."

"Ya, they have chicken, but they eat it themselves and give you only the wing." Thanks to Fanča's honesty, I avoided accepting a terrible job.

The Munk family

My first truly permanent job in Jablonec was with the Munk family. They were a Jewish couple with no children. The wife had a married brother about forty who also had no children. One Saturday, after I had been working there for awhile, the brother and his wife came over for a visit. They were very friendly to me. In fact, they seemed to like me a lot. The next week, the brother came alone. My employer wasn't at home, which I soon realized wasn't by accident. The brother sat down on the sofa and invited me to sit next to him. Something warned me not to trust him. I grabbed a basket and ran out yelling, "I have to put this in the room across the hall." Although I was dressed lightly, I ran out of the house into the freezing air. I knew that madam was probably in town, so I went to search for her. I found her in a shop nearby, and we walked back to the house together. Speaking softly, she confided, "You know, Toni, they want so much to have a child." She explained that her brother would like to have a child with me, and then he and his wife would adopt it. Thank God my guardian angel stayed with me, or maybe my mother's spirit protected me. I had only been at the house for a few months when this incident happened. I stayed on until the summer. They didn't need me after that; their cleaning maid was enough. Anyway, I didn't mind leaving. The Munks didn't feed me much, so I was always hungry.

I thought I was done with them, but I was wrong. Not long after, when I was working at my next job, they sent a messenger to fetch me. The apprentice from the sweets shop told me that some people were waiting to see me. They turned out to be the Munks. They begged me to come back and told me they needed me, even through the summer months. I refused. No matter what they promised, I vowed I would never work in their house again.

Later, I heard that they ended up in a German concentration camp. It seems like that's what happened to all the Jewish people I knew.

Jablonec in 1922

At that time, I was living with my next employer, the Janovskýs. They had a six-story house on Údolní Street with a jewelry-making shop on the ground floor and their own living quarters on the second floor. They rented out the apartments on the upper floors.

Jára, let me give you an idea of the layout of the neighborhood so you can picture in your mind the streets, shops, and general vicinity where I lived, worked, shopped, and walked nearly every day. To the right of the Janovský house was a bakery shop, three houses, and then a butcher shop. At that time, all the shop signs in Jablonec were in German.

The railroad tracks ran behind our street. In front, and alongside our street, was the Nisa River where I used to go to rinse and whiten the laundry. Across the bridge on the other side of the river was a big meadow of grass and gravel with some swings for the children to play on. Sometimes this area was used by the circus that came to town or for other events needing a large, open space. Behind this meadow were two eleven-story apartment buildings that we called skyscrapers. To the right of the skyscrapers were seventy-eight steps that led up to the Exhibition Pavilion and the Protestant Church on Podhorská, the main street.

A short distance from the church (where the new city hall now stands), there used to be an open-air market. I remember buying myself a jacket at that market. At various stalls, vendors sold fruit, vegetables, butter, and poultry. I went there to shop every Friday with Madam Janovská. Whenever I passed by the sweet shop, I stopped at the large window to stare at the inviting treats inside. Another one of my favorite spots was the Czech restaurant where I went every day for a beer.

The post office was on the street now called Liberecká. Opposite the post office was a theater. A little further on was the Munk's house; I don't remember the street name. If you walk along Liberecká, on the right was a hospital and a cemetery. There was also a gasworks.

The part of town where Julča and Máňa worked

Julča served in a house near the Protestant Church. She was a maid for a Jewish family. The house had lots of rats, which scared Julča out of her wits. Every time she went into the laundry room in the cellar, rats jumped over her feet. So she quit and found another position near the railroad station, but she just traded one nuisance for another. She slept in a small room in the attic which was fine, except it was full of bedbugs. Máňa found Julča another job, this time with a family who lived behind the dam. She worked there for almost a year, although she didn't live with this family. Instead, she moved into a clean apartment with two roommates. With the three of them sharing expenses, they could afford a better place to live.

The following year, a man stopped me when I was standing in a small shop near the Janovský house. "Where is Julča working now?" he asked.

"Julča moved," I told him. "She's working in Bratislava." That man was Emil, Julča's future husband. Many people were unemployed at that time, but Emil was fortunate. He had a job delivering bread for his uncle, a baker in Lišný.

My sister, Máňa, was already married; however, that didn't make her life any easier. Máňa worked in a factory on Gutenbergstrasse ten hours a day, five days a week plus a half-day on Saturdays. She carried her lunch with her; there were no cafeterias then. She walked a long distance to the factory every day, and in winter it was still dark and cold when she left home. She had to walk about 800 meters along Dlouhá Street, climb the hill past City Hall, and cross Pastaj Square, where there was a new church. After Pastaj Square, the final challenge was the dam. It wasn't much of a problem in sunny weather, but crossing the narrow bridge was a curse during heavy rain and winds. She had a much harder life than I did, at least while I was working at the Janovskýs.

The Janovskýs

I was very happy at the Janovskýs. (But stupid me, I got married soon and that was the end of a worry-free life.)

Marie, the lady of the house, was a young, Christian Czech, a hat maker by trade. Her Jakub was a handsome man, tall and thin. Even though he was Jewish, he had a normal nose. In the early days before she and Jakub Janovský were married, she used to help out in Jakub's millinery shop located in the ground floor of his house. At that time, her living quarters were in one of the upstairs rooms.

After their romance got going, Marie joined him in his apartment. That's when I started working for them.

Even though they weren't yet married, I called her *madam* and greeted her in the manner I did all women of higher social rank—"Merciful lady, I kiss your hand." I also used to call the man of the house, *the lord*. The lord and his son (from a previous marriage) owned and managed the costume jewelry shop.

The Janovskýs had pet names for each other. Jakub called his wife Mitzi and she called him Schatzi, although their real names were Marie and Jakub. Before they were married, they got along well together. Afterwards, madam began to make demands on him; once they even stopped talking to each other.

When Marie and Jakub decided to get married, they chose Switzerland as the place for their wedding ceremony. (Every year after that, they returned for their vacation.) When they got back from their honeymoon, Marie's mother came to visit the newlyweds with another one of her daughters. We all had a big feast. I don't remember everything that there was to eat and drink, but I do recall that a confectioner came and made vanilla-flavored ice cream. I was eighteen, and it was the first time I ever tasted ice cream.

It was Jakub's custom to go to the coffee house every day after lunch. Sometimes his wife and I accompanied him in case he needed something. He always liked to dress elegantly. I know, because I had lots of his shirts to launder.

The Janovskýs were good to me. Sometimes Jakub would come into the kitchen and sing a special song to me in Czech (about the sun shining down on a ramshackle cottage), *Roztrhaná chalupa, slunce do ní svícáááá*. Jakub was Polish by birth and never learned to speak Czech very well. He prolonged the last sound a bit too long, but he didn't know better.

He started to lose his health during the time I was working there. His doctor told him to stick to a special low-fat diet, but his wife didn't cooperate. She didn't understand how important the diet was for her husband's health. They always ate rich, imported food. To her, if a food was tasty and expensive, it had to be healthy. She couldn't see how it could hurt. So every week, the lord and lady ate goose liver in lard, and in spring, young Italian goose with cucumber salad and new potatoes. On work days, there was veal, chicken, fish, young beef, and sometimes even pork. The lord made an exception, once in awhile, because of madam. Jews don't eat pork. That was something I learned (though I think some do today).

Sometimes the lord ordered smoked sausages from Hungary. They were so big, I could hardly eat a whole one. What they ate, I ate. Boiled potatoes weren't the main dish in this house as it was when I was growing up. At the Janovský family table, potatoes were only a side dish to the meat. We each had one potato; the rest was meat—one kind for lunch and a different kind for dinner.

In 1922, there were no refrigerators yet in Czechoslovakia, so food was stored in the basement. Basements were deep and cold. They had two parts: one for storage of coal, the other for food. The milk I purchased for the Janovskýs, from a German farmer in Rychnov, stayed fresh one full week in their basement.

Summer jobs

I took advantage of the month that the Janovskýs were vacationing in Switzerland to return home to Rovensko. Every morning, I got up early to help with the farm chores. I fed the chickens, milked the goats, and took the goats to pasture. I also did laundry and carried water from the well below the hill. Then I cut the grass and assisted wherever I was needed. I used to go with my stepmother to a nearby garden to work side-by-side with her in a farmer's small vegetable patch. The farmer paid her, but she never offered me anything for my help with the garden work. I never expected her to pay me anything for assisting her with farm chores, but working for someone else was different. Why didn't she see that?

Sometimes I went beyond Trosky to gather firewood. It was a long time since I had carried firewood and I hurt my back trying to manage a bundle much too big for me. My stepmother expected me to do everything for her. The next vacation, I decided not to return home.

At harvest time, I took a job at the mill, but a straw got into my finger and it became inflamed. When I was supposed to go back to Jablonec to my house-cleaning job, the finger was still infected. Madam Janovská wrote asking me why I hadn't returned yet. Finally I did go back, but my finger throbbed and it was difficult for me to do my chores.

Other years when the Janovskýs were away on vacation, I accepted various summer jobs. I couldn't afford not to. One summer, I served in the home of a Jewish family named Fisher who lived near the dam. I was very fond of their big German Shepherd. Many years later, during the German occupation, I talked with Fisher again. He told me that the family planned to flee to England, but I don't know if they ever reached there.

Another year, I worked for three weeks as a maid at Novák's house. He was a shoemaker. His workshop was in the yard of the local Protestant Church. When he first started out, your Uncle Konůpek used to work for him; he even lived at Novák's home. My summer job earned me 150 crowns, which in those days was worth about one pair of shoes or 300 chocolate bars (your favorite unit of measurement, Jára, when you were a boy).

Novák had a hard life. It's not surprising that he stuttered; he had to cope with so many difficulties. He had four children, one of them still in a stroller. His wife was in such poor health, she could barely prepare lunch for us. What she did serve us was bad, and there was very little of it. Novák said that the maid before me ate too much. I got the hint and ate only the bare minimum. I was constantly at the washtub scrubbing the laundry. To rinse, I had to lug the wet wash to the Nisa River where it flowed below the dam. On my way back, I struggled to keep my balance climbing up the steep hill with a heavy basket of laundry.

At that time, shoes were made by hand; only the tops were made by machine. Novák was skilled at his trade, but one thing I can tell you for sure is that he wasn't a businessman. Jablonec's German population never came into his shop and the few Czechs who were his customers didn't order enough to keep his business going. He took out many loans and finally went bankrupt (but that was after I left).

Novák owned a small house near Smržovka which he burned down to collect the insurance money. When he was challenged in court, he admitted to starting the fire, so he didn't collect anything.

The innkeepers

While I was working at the Janovskýs, I went every evening to a German inn and restaurant for a glass of beer. The woman innkeeper had a son who was always after me. Every time I entered the restaurant, he immediately came over and sat down next to me and begged in his whiney voice, "Pretty girl, kiss?" That's all the Czech he knew. His mother had to chase him away from me. I complained about him to Madam Janovská.

"Go get your beer at the Czech restaurant," she replied impatiently.

The Czech restaurant was further away, but I tried going there hoping to avoid the lecherous men who were always after me. One day, while I was waiting for my beer, one of the patrons walked over to me and introduced himself. He soon took me by the hand and brought me over to the table where his friends, all Moravians, were sitting. They admired my beautiful eyes, teeth and hair. My hair was truly beautiful. I had two braids thrown over my shoulders. (I remember when I was still a child living at home with my parents, a barber offered my father ten Austro-Hungarian *gilders* for my braids. *Tatínek* discussed the offer with *maminka*, and before I knew it, I was at the barber shop. But I cried so hard that we returned home with my hair intact. Ten gilders was big money, and it would have really helped our family. I was a foolish kid then. I don't know why I made such a fuss.)

The main problem at the Czech restaurant was the innkeeper himself who couldn't keep his hands off me. His wife had recently become an invalid following a terrible childbirth experience. The child survived only a short time. His wife, now unable to walk, spent her days lying in bed or sitting on a couch.

On a particular Saturday afternoon, I was sitting all alone in the restaurant with not even a waiter around. That horny innkeeper came over to me and, like in a bad dream, started to kiss me. I pulled away. Luckily for me, a patron entered, and the innkeeper stopped his assault. Again I complained to my lady about the problem. Her solution was to send me back to the German restaurant. The innkeeper's son was, at that time, in jail for attempted murder. He was arrested because he went berserk at a church wedding and shot the groom, who was to be his mother's new husband. I wasn't particularly surprised. A person like he was bound to end up in jail.

Some time later, I stopped in again at the German restaurant. To my dismay, the innkeeper's son was back. He had got off easy because the victim wasn't badly hurt. As soon as he noticed me, he walked right over; he sat down next to me and began his old tricks. He had learned a few more Czech words and used them to try to seduce me into sleeping at his place. "I'll give you the nicest room in the inn," he coaxed.

"I have a place to sleep, thank you," I snapped back.

The end of the Janovskýs

Shortly after I left the Janovskýs, Jakub passed away. At his funeral, their Jewish friends and family threw small change into his grave so that he would have money for his trip to the afterlife. Marie inherited 80,000 crowns and a great deal of property. She found herself a boyfriend who helped her spend the money. They even managed to get into debt.

Later, Marie married Jirásek, the owner of a print shop in Turnov. He had a lovely villa. How she managed to marry a rich man again, I'll never know. She wasn't a beauty, just an ordinary woman. Jirásek was already an older man, fat and a head shorter than she. The last time I talked to her was in front of the elementary school in Turnov. It was 1934, and I was on my way to register you for classes. Shortly afterwards, I heard she died while eating at her favorite restaurant. She had a stroke just as she was finishing a plate of goose liver. I read the obituary in the newspaper. It included all of her names, the history of her marriages: Vonostránská, Janovská, Jirásková.

Not long after that, I had a conversation with Marie's sister. She told me that she was going to marry her brother-in-law, the widower. She became the fourth Jirásková. People began talking about how he liquidated his wives, how marrying him was the kiss of death.

The end of my single life

In the summer of 1923, during my single days, I used to go dancing with your father and his friends at a second Czech restaurant (not the one I mentioned earlier). It was on Ustunggasse, the hilly street near Údolní where I lived. Your father would walk me back to the Janovský villa at the end of the evening. We lived in the same direction, his home being a little further down the road.

Coincidentally, one evening when your father and I were sitting at our favorite restaurant, the innkeeper from the other Czech restaurant, on Údolní Street, came in and sat down next to us. It was obvious that he was curious about who I was with. That was the last time I saw the innkeeper. In February of the following year, I got married—the end of my freedom.

Chapter 5
Wife and Mother

Jára's background notes
First Republic continues: 1924-1928

My mother was unprepared for the radical changes in her life that came with marriage and a family. She was accustomed to making do with very little, but survival for a young single woman was much simpler than the sacrifices required for a wife and mother.

Typically, Bohemian mothers, before moving to another city to work, made arrangements to leave their infants for extended periods of time with friends and family back home. These caretakers were paid whatever the parents could afford.

Leaving children behind was a difficult decision, but bringing them along presented other problems. City life meant living in conditions that were even more cramped than those in their home towns. Additionally, child care was less reliable and harder to find for a young mother unfamiliar with city life.

As Mother's letter describes, husbands too, had to live close to wherever they found work. Everybody was compelled to follow the jobs, even if this meant splitting up the family. Only after a couple jointly accumulated enough money to afford a decent-sized apartment could a husband and wife make some arrangement to unite the family, assuming that both could then find jobs in the same vicinity. One solution was to find a way for the wife to work at home. But sometimes this solution came too late, leaving families scarred and, in today's parlance, dysfunctional.

I didn't live with my father when I was very young. I lived with the Vondras, family friends of my mother in Rovensko. When I came to live with my own mother and father in 1927, I was already two years old. My father resented my intrusion in his life and beat me in frustration. I always had bruises or welts on the top or back of my head, his favorite places to hit me. We had a bad relationship, and those beatings were a large part of what destroyed any possibility of warmth between us.

I understood beatings as discipline because, in those days, most parents in Czechoslovakia hit their kids to teach them obedience. What got me mad was that my father beat me unjustly. I remember one instance very clearly. I was playing intently with my toy train on top of our general purpose table. I loved my train set; it was my favorite toy. Suddenly, my father ordered me to remove it from the table. I started to gather up the train pieces, but I didn't move quickly enough for him, so he angrily smashed them to the floor and beat me with his belt.

My mother tried to make excuses for the way he treated me. In recent years, she wrote me in her letters, "Your father didn't like you because he wasn't used to you. Since he didn't have the opportunity to know you as a baby, he never developed a paternal bond with you." As she also reminded me, he was ill during most of my childhood. But these excuses didn't change how I felt about him.

I lived in Jablonec from ages two to nine. Our first apartment there consisted of one room where our family of four slept and ate crowded together. It was an underground, cell-like apartment, below street level, that gave me the feeling of living in a cage. I had to climb up a dark stairway from the basement just to reach the building's front door. (On the positive side, since the upper half of our front window was above street level, I was still small enough, at age six, to crawl out the top part of the window and onto the street.) Nevertheless, on the whole, it was not a good living environment for raising a young family with two active boys, and this no doubt added to the tension between my father and me.

Our next apartment in Jablonec was in a building exclusively for state employees, an entitlement that came with my father's job at the Post Office. We had a large kitchen and bedroom area, plus an outside balcony. The apartment was big in terms of square feet, but in reality, it was only a one-bedroom flat with no partitions. In older houses, it was not uncommon to have a lot of space like that. In the center of the apartment, we had a long hall that led to the w.c.. Getting a toilet and balcony was big progress for us.

Jablonec was a substantial city with a population of about 34,000 with approximately eighty percent German, seventeen percent Czech, and a few percent others.[27] Even though we were Czechs in our own country, we were a minority in Jablonec. Since the city was mostly German, my first social contacts growing up in Jablonec were with Germans rather than Czechs. When I was little, I didn't feel any differences between me and my German playmates. I got those feelings later when, at the age of six, we moved to the apartment for state employees.

Although the new neighborhood, as a whole, had the same high ratio of Germans to Czechs as any other part of the city, our apartment building complex was unique. Everyone who lived there was Czech. There were enough families in that building to provide me with all my friends. In this environment, I lost contact with the German population and correspondingly lost my ability to speak fluent German.

In Jablonec, there were separate schools for Czechs and Germans. It was the custom in Czechoslovakia for boys and girls to go to separate schools, too. The city had several German schools to accommodate their boys and girls, but only one each for the Czech children. It was at the segregated Czech school for boys that I started my education.

From the time I moved to the new neighborhood, the gulf continually widened between the Germans and Czechs. The German kids threw stones at us in the streets and we threw them back. Sometimes, on our way home from school, they tried to prevent us from passing. Often we had to fight our way through their blockades. Other skirmishes occurred because of language difficulties and the bitter feelings that were growing every day. These struggles began to take place on a daily basis. We Czechs were fewer in number, so we were beaten quite often.

When I was about nine years old, I got fed up with the way the German kids were terrorizing us. One day, I walked over to the police station. There was a Czech policeman patrolling outside in front of the building. I complained to him, "The German kids are always beating us and throwing stones at us." All he did was try to pacify me. I was just a little boy and the policeman was a stern authority figure. I didn't get much sympathy from him. He may have thought that I was sincere, but he didn't take me seriously. He hadn't seen the fighting and didn't recognize the problem. Or maybe he himself was intimidated by the large German population. I've always felt that he probably wasn't aware of the animosity that was growing in the city. Maybe no one was. Later on, during the German Occupation, I thought back to these earlier times and compared them to life under the Occupation. It bothered me that, if it had been the other way around, with Czech kids beating up the German kids, the German police would not have ignored their complaints. They certainly would have punished us.

As the Germans in Czechoslovakia began to identify more and more with Germany, they became more and more hostile. In those early years (maybe 1932-34), it seems as though the ethnic Germans in the borderlands were preparing psychologically to connect up with Germany. There was a movement building that we weren't aware of. But it was still five years before the Occupation and WWII. We were not worrying about Germany at that time.

In hindsight, it is now clear that there were two distinct ethnic groups in the districts of Bohemia and Moravia—the Czechs and the Germans—and each hated the other. It wasn't always that way, but over the years the hatred grew. I felt these tensions every day in my daily life until 1934, when we moved from Jablonec to Daliměřice. In the following letter, my mother discusses life with my father and the difficulties raising a family during those troubled years prior to my father's death.

Tonča's letter to Jára

Papa and I got married in Jablonec on February of 1924, before my nineteenth birthday. We didn't give the question of marriage a lot of thought. One day we just did it. I owned nothing except a few articles of clothing and knew almost nothing about homemaking outside of cleaning and laundry chores. I didn't even know how to cook. As a maid, I didn't need to. The lady of the house did the cooking. Even if I knew how, I still couldn't have prepared anything hot because Papa and I couldn't afford a pot. Instead, we ate simple foods that required no heating, like bologna, cheese and bread—whatever a few crowns could buy.

At that time, we were extremely poor. I was young and terribly in love; I thought our love was all we needed for a blissful married life. It is painful to remember the many mistakes I made in my ignorance—mistakes that I regret today.

Our marriage ceremony took place in a post office building that had a little social hall available for such occasions. Jablonec is cold and wet in winter, and those old buildings were poorly heated and didn't protect us much from the freezing temperatures outside. It was so chilly inside that I needed to keep my coat on during the ceremony. I was happy to do so because my warm, brown coat was newer and prettier than the simple dress I was wearing. Besides, that coat was a gift from your papa—the first coat I ever had.

In addition to the city official who conducted the wedding ceremony, the only people present were my sister, Máňa, and another witness who I don't remember today. After we exchanged vows, we walked to a small restaurant nearby that prepared a Czech soup that was popular at the time. It consisted mainly of small strips of stomach lining called tripe. This soup was one of the cheapest meals we could buy, but it was also very tasty. (Later on, Papa and I would sometimes go to a butcher shop for this soup and eat it standing there on the spot.) Our wedding day over, we caught the train home and got off at Turnov. It was our way of saving money—walking the rest of the way to Rovensko. On the road, we met a farmer heading in our direction who let us ride with him in his horse-drawn carriage. But a passing train panicked his horse and the carriage turned over, throwing us all into a ditch. Unhurt, we picked ourselves up and completed the rest of our journey on foot, about five miles more.

My life as a married woman was now underway. As luck would have it, I experienced little joy in this role. Part of my problem was I didn't know how to grab on to opportunities or mold life to my advantage. Jára, because of your father's illness and early death, my marriage was short and not too happy. We had only ten years together.

A room for two

After a while, your papa managed to get a little room for the two of us in an attic apartment. Living in that freezing room, it wasn't surprising that he caught pneumonia. In fact, he got sick many times while we were living there. I remember a night during the first year of our marriage when his fever rose to 40° C [104° F]. He recovered from that illness, but he never really regained his health. All in all, he wasn't a healthy man, even when I first married him.

There was a big apartment shortage in Jablonec at that time, so we were grateful to find that attic apartment. Papa was earning 600 crowns per month. The landlord demanded a down payment of 1000 crowns; on top of that, we paid monthly rent of 100 crowns. That was big money in those days.

In the winter, the water froze in the downstairs communal washtub. We had only a small, sheet-metal stove that we used for warming our room. The shared toilet and sink were on the first floor. The way we got our water was to carry it from the sink up the two flights of stairs to the third floor. There we rested for a minute, then lugged the heavy pail the rest of the way up the steep, narrow stairway to our room. I don't remember exactly how long we stayed in that attic room waiting for an apartment to become available.

A baby coming

When I was pregnant with you, I went with your Aunt Máňa to visit a fortuneteller on Bamberg Hill. It was a beautiful day. We enjoyed our stroll through the forest and even found some mushrooms to pick on the way. At the fortuneteller, we spent a few minutes in pleasant conversation, then the woman told me, "You will live until a very old age and will suffer a painful loss in 1933." She missed that date by only four days. Your father died January 4, 1934. Then she said, "You will have three children." The fortuneteller would have been right if not for my one miscarriage. She continued, "Your first born will be a boy," which, of course, was you. Well, I only laughed. I didn't take her seriously but as it turned out, everything she told me came true.

When I was ready to give birth, I moved from Jablonec back to my childhood home in Rovensko. I delivered you there all alone, without any help. It's not surprising that I tore. It was terribly painful. My father went for a doctor to sew me up, but he arrived hours after you were born. (With your brother, Mirek, everything was fine because I had help.)

Your first year

Papa wasn't present at your baptism. It was my father, not Papa, who bought the bottle of cumin brandy we drank to celebrate your birth. I only got a taste because my stepmother invited her three sons and her sister, and the brandy disappeared before I knew it. Your godmother was our neighbor, Kožená , who was also my godmother and maybe the godmother of all of us. Her daughter brought me a big cake. Grandma Masáková sent a piece of smoked meat and a pillow.

My father and stepmother let me stay with them in their one-room cottage in Rovensko for the first two months after you were born. During that time, you cried almost all night, keeping my poor parents from getting any sleep. You probably were terribly overheated; I had you wrapped up in a tight bundle. I'm sure the stuffy air in our tiny cottage didn't help either. *Tatínek* smoked a pipe, and once in a while another neighbor, who was also a smoker, came to visit him. The neighbor smoked a long pipe that reached down to the floor. How you must have suffered trying to get a good breath in all that bad air!

One evening, my parents went out visiting. You were sleeping well, and I fell into a very deep slumber making up for many nights of little sleep. When my folks returned later that night, the house was all locked up, so they couldn't get in. My father finally thought to get a ladder. He climbed through the attic window and opened the door for his wife from inside the house. They had just gotten into bed when you started crying. I woke up immediately, only to hear my stepmother grumble, "I knew it. Now Tonča wakes up!" It was a sacrifice for them. They didn't have it easy with me, but youth is selfish.

After the two months stay with my parents was up, our neighbor, Kudibálová, accepted you and me into her apartment. She was a very nice woman. We lived in the room with the machine that Kudibálová used during the day to grind garnets. When the apartment downstairs became available, she moved the grinder in there and we had the room for ourselves. But we really weren't alone. Huge field mice shared the room with us. Once, as I was climbing out of my bath, I saw one of the mice drowned in the tub. I bought poisoned grain and poured it around the bottom of the walls in our room, which worked to get rid of them.

Unfortunately, Jára, you were born under very difficult circumstances. At the beginning of our marriage, Papa and I really couldn't afford a family and had to live separately. We both had to work and live near wherever we could find jobs. Also, we couldn't afford to rent a whole apartment. So I either lived in a rented room or in the home of my employer. Papa lived in Jablonec in a dormitory with five other men. When you were eight months old, you went to live with the Vondras, who were the parents of one of my girlfriends. We paid them half of your father's salary for your care.

With you safely placed with the Vondras, I came back to live and work in Jablonec to be closer to Papa. I moved in with Máňa's sister-in-law, a semi-invalid, who required personal and household help. She also needed as many people as possible to help her share the rent. My contribution wasn't only rent money. I had to do all the laundry and cleaning for her and for me, as well as for the four students who also shared the apartment. During this time, I was working a ten-hour day on weekdays, plus Saturday morning, at a factory where I operated a drill press. The flying particles of hot metal often left me with burns on my face and neck. I was exhausted at the end of the day. Yet, despite how I felt, when I came home I had to do all those household chores.

In 1927, your papa and I found our first apartment. Our friends in Jablonec had moved to Říčany and vacated the apartment they had been renting from Řanda, the landlord. Places were still scarce, so we felt very lucky to get their old apartment. Papa and I purchased our furniture and other household articles on installment from a special store for state employees in Praha. (We could shop there because Papa was a post office employee.) Your father also bought me a gold chain from that store. I loved it, but I told him, "I'd be afraid to wear it—what if I lost it?" So he exchanged it for comforters and a tablecloth.

We also bought three plates, two pots, and a baking dish for cooking and eating. We could now eat hot food. Our stove was very important to us, but it also could be a nuisance, or even deadly. One day, I noticed that our stovepipe was clogged with soot and needed cleaning out. Always looking for a short cut, I filled the pipe with newspapers, poured kerosine over them, and threw in a lit match. Boom! I heard a blast like thunder from the kerosine igniting the soot. The lids from the pots flew like missiles, and soot covered everything.

In those days, apartment buildings often had one central pipe inside the chimney that all the individual apartment stove pipes tapped into. Such a design was illegal, but builders did it anyway since there were few inspectors to enforce regulations. Nowadays each apartment has its own pipe outlet so mistakes or carelessness by one tenant will not affect the others. But then it was different. In my case, the blast not only shot soot back into our apartment, it also blew the soot up into the central pipe and then branched out into the three other apartment ducts that were hooked into the same chimney pipe.

Fortunately, no one else was home at the time except the landlady's grandmother. When the landlady finally arrived home and saw the mess, she said, "You are lucky that the explosion didn't destroy the Dutch oven [tile stove]. You would have had to pay dearly for that." I cleaned both my apartment and the landlady's. The other tenants cleaned their own places.

Actually, it wasn't strange for an explosion like that to happen. Everyone knew the danger of having too much soot blocking the air flow. But people often cut corners like I did and suffered disastrous results.

Family life

My luck soon improved. I was able to find an employer who allowed me to work at home making costume jewelry right there in our Jablonec apartment. Afterwards, I carried the completed jewelry from our apartment back to my employer's shop behind the dam. The heavy handbags with the jewelry made the journey feel longer than it actually was. Along the way, I would pass through the town square. In the square was a small wooden platform, and often it was the center of attention with people waiting their turn to speak. Even a heavy snowfall wouldn't discourage one hundred or so people from waiting patiently to hear what the speakers had to say about the popular topics of the day: low wages, unemployment, and the high cost of living.

With me working from home, we were now able to have you come live with us. I remember buying you your first pants outfit. You were two years old. Before then, you wore only girl's clothing. It was the custom to dress babies like that because of convenience and the poor sanitation in those days.

I cried with joy and sadness, mostly sadness, on the day I took you back from your foster parents to live with Papa and me. I wanted you with us, but I also knew it was hard for you to break away from Ema and Pepa. The Vondras were an older couple with grown-up children, a son and a daughter. *Páčík* and *Aňa* you called them in baby talk. I remember, you whispered softly to me on the way home, "Aňa's gone, Páčík's gone, all gone." How lonely you were! I cry and I cry when I think of that time when I gave you to the Vondra family to raise. How miserable I felt having to leave you in the care of someone else when you were so young. I have lived with that pain every day of my life. It's a shame that those days can't be relived and that only bitter memories remain.

Your father had a terrible temper, sometimes even towards me. I know he spanked you many times unjustly. I don't remember ever spanking you. The way he treated you led to many quarrels. Papa never bonded with you or accepted you as a father naturally would. That was because he didn't know you as a baby. When you came to live with us, he saw you just as an annoying brat, under his feet, disturbing his peace and quiet. You had a sad childhood. It hurt me so much that he rejected you. When I look back, I see that my marriage made no sense at all.

Games of pretend

When you were a young child, one of your favorite activities was "reading" the newspaper. You would sit on the sofa with the newspaper open in front of you and make up stories as if you were reading them in the paper. You also enjoyed visiting the tailor's son who lived on the second floor. From his apartment window, you and your little friend could watch the trains passing by and play games of pretend.

"I sat on top of the train," you told me. "The engine whistled, and the steam came out."

Years later, Jára, that same tailor hanged himself. Our elderly landlady also died from unnatural causes. She turned on the gas stove and suffocated when the oxygen in the room ran out. We thought it was an accident; maybe it was, maybe it wasn't.

One winter in Jablonec, you and your friends built an eight-foot-high snow castle. The fresh snow made nice blocks and was moist enough to pack down and stick together. You were the chief engineer and architect on that project. Before the boys started putting the blocks in place, you drew up the plans showing where the walls for each of the three rooms were to be built and where the windows and doors should go. The boys followed your plan. The high walls that opened to the sky were quite impressive. At that time, you dreamed of becoming an architect when you grew up. Although you didn't, you really had a flair for that kind of thing.

When we lived in Daliměřice, you built other castles with the fine sand left by the builders who had built our house. With a little water, you found you could mold the soft moist sand into castles like the Trosky Ruins near your grandfather's house.

An unexpected farewell gift

During the time we were living at Řanda's place, 1927-1931, Jablonec was overrun with *Egerlanders*, who were a source of cheap labor for the factories in the area. These people, from several isolated mountain communities, came down to the city to find work. They spoke a peculiar German dialect that set them apart from both Czechs and other Germans, so it wasn't easy for them. Our landlord's wife, a Czech, who knew some German, accepted two of these Egerlanders as lodgers, fortunately for them. Around that time, Papa and I accepted an offer from the government to move into a new housing development for state employees. Since affordable apartments were difficult to come by, we were particularly happy for the opportunity. The day before we left, one of the Egerlander women gave me a complete dinner—pork, dumplings and kraut—as a farewell gift. She said something to me in her dialect. I didn't understand a single word she said, but I will never forget her kindness.

Chapter 6
Husband and Father

Jára's background notes
First Republic continues: 1924-1934

Mother writes about my father whose formal education, like that of most people in their community, lasted until he was about ten years old—the end of elementary school. She then returns to the topic of my father's eventual employment by the post office. Those who managed to get a job in the government were fortunate. They received a retirement pension and, in the case of death, their widows were entitled to a pension if their husbands had served the required number of years. Having a guaranteed income was of immense value to a widow because women had few decent job opportunities.

A person holding a government job was held in high regard in the community. In case of disputes, his (most would be men) arguments carried extra weight. There were also valuable perks that came with these jobs, like a flat in an apartment complex available only to government employees, out-of-town conferences, and paid vacations. For all these reasons, my mother was very grateful that my father had worked for the post office.

At the end of this letter, my mother writes of my father's death. I remember how I heard that he was dead. It was during my third grade religion class. The teacher who taught the class was a priest who wore clerical attire. My Uncle Konůpek suddenly appeared in the doorway of my class and walked straight over to him. He whispered something to the priest and then turned around and walked out. The priest faced the class and told us that he had an announcement to make. He told the class that my father had died and instructed the children to stand and pray for my father's soul. I stood, but I didn't pray. The rest of the day went as usual with me attending my regular sequence of classes. After school was over, some of my friends expressed their sympathy as we were walking home together. I said, "I'm glad he died. He's not going to beat me anymore."

Tonča's letter to Jára

There were many mysteries in my life. For example, why did I fall in love with your father? As it happened, his pension brought financial security to my later years, but I didn't expect that when I married him. I had more luck than brains.

I knew who your father was before he discovered me. Once, when I was walking to the butcher's, he ran right by me and almost knocked me to the ground. His cap fell off and he had to stop and pick it up, but he didn't notice me. Another time, on Údolní Street where I used to walk on my way to get my daily beer, your father and a co-worker were driving by in the mail buggy. It was his buddy who told him to take a look at the beautiful girl walking by. The first time we actually met was on St. Anna Day at the fair in Vrkoslavice when your father asked me to dance. We had one dance together that day.

Papa's life

Your father's life and death were both difficult. When he was twelve, his stepfather chased him out of the house shouting, "Go find a job somewhere." He soon found work helping a farmer in Boseň. Papa used to tell me how much he had to do before setting off for school each morning. In later years, he fought in World War I in the Karpaten Mountains, where the winters were miserably cold. Wearing only thin cloth shoes, he suffered from frost-bitten feet. Just before your father's term in the military was up in 1919, they offered him a position in the police unit serving in Karpaten-Ukrajine, near the far eastern border. His response was a quick, "No thanks." It is interesting that Papa started his military service under the Emperor, and ended his service in the Czech military.

During the first year of our marriage, Papa was called back for four weeks of refresher military training at Kutná Hora, a remote area that was formerly a silver-mining district. Because of its mineral wealth, Kutná Hora had been second only to Praha in importance in medieval Bohemia. "You have to see this beautiful place," Papa said when he returned. I promised him I would some day. I kept my word many years later after his death. I went there with a group of tourists.

Delivering the mail

By the time we were married in 1924, Papa had already worked five years as a horse driver for Dolánský Delivery Service. In the early twenties, there weren't many cars yet and the horse and buggy business flourished. Dolánský had all sorts of wagons in the yard: cargo, light passenger carriages, moving wagons, and postal wagons. The horses were lodged inside the stables, so the yard where the wagons were kept was always clean.

The company employed seven drivers. Your father drove every day carrying mail to Rychnov. When he returned to Dolánský's at the end of the day, he spent the night in a big room downstairs with the other drivers. They had only straw mattresses to sleep on, one after the other in a row. A chair and a stove completed the room furnishings—there was nothing else. The men hung their clothing on nails.

One Sunday, I drove with Papa to the post office in Kokonín where he stopped the carriage to pick up the head postmaster, his wife, and another woman. I chatted with the women all the way to Český Dub. It was obvious they all liked me. As we were driving along, the head postmaster said to Papa, "If only you had a high school education. If you did, I could get you a government job as postmaster in some small village post office." Nevertheless, the head postmaster was able to convince the director of the Jablonec Post Office to hire your papa as an assistant. They must have realized that although your father had only a grade school education, he was an intelligent, able man.

In 1926, Papa moved up from postal assistant to mail carrier. On his route, in a secluded spot next to a cemetery, was a villa guarded by two big dogs. One day, as your father was making his rounds, one of the dogs attacked him. The dog tore away his pants and left deep scratches on his leg. The dog's owner begged Papa not to report the incident and gave him 300 crowns to keep quiet. Since that was a tidy sum, your father took the money and never made trouble for the man.

Good times and tough times

With a better salary coming in, your father was able to buy me a pair of light brown, high-heeled shoes for twenty-nine crowns. It was 1928. I remember those shoes because it was so unusual for me, in the 1920s, to get new, leather dress shoes.

Our coal was delivered in sacks by horse-drawn wagons. Customers would stop the wagon and pay the deliveryman for the amount they wanted. Because the winter of 1929 was unusually cold, the coal was sold out before the wagon would normally reach our house. When the coal wagon didn't come, I had no choice but to collect the coal myself. I took a sack and a shovel and went to the coal warehouse at the railroad station where it was okay to serve yourself. Although I was eight months pregnant with your brother, Mirek, I hacked up the coal and struggled to drag the full twenty five kg [fifty five pound] sack and my big belly back up the steep hill to where we lived.

I have fond memories of going with your father to a movie theater. We saw one of the first movies with sound in 1932—a musical comedy, *C.A.K. Polní Maršálek* [Imperial Royal Field Marshal, a Czech film released in 1930] starring Vasta Burian. I was so happy having Papa seated next to me. I felt a wonderful sense of security. We had very little money then, but we enjoyed being together, holding hands as we walked down the street or taking short hikes into the countryside. Other times, we just sat together at the inn, having our beers and sometimes joining the other dancers on the small dance floor.

In 1933, there was a convention of post office employees in Praha. Two buses drove in from Jablonec, and we were in one of them. It was a hot day; I think it was June. We walked all day exploring the streets of Praha. We climbed to the top of Petřín Hill and gazed down at the lovely view of the city. Coming down the hill, we admired the beautiful homes on both sides of the street. I was used to walking on dirt streets, not cement sidewalks and cobblestone roads. Jára, can you imagine how much my feet hurt? I finally got some relief when I was able to stick my feet in the Vltava River. Later that day when we visited my aunt in Žižkov, I soaked them in a pail of cold water. How soothing it felt to my tortured feet!

The fly

In early spring after the treacherous winter of 1929, your papa and I decided to get out and enjoy a little hiking in the mountains with our friends, the Janoušeks. We left you and Mirek behind with your Aunt Julča.

Your visit with her was a disaster, Jára. Do you remember why? Maybe you do, because you upset Aunt Julča so much. The summer before, a fly flew into your aunt and uncle's small apartment and stayed. Somehow it survived the fall and winter and miraculously lived way past the normal life span you would expect of flies. To your aunt, the fly became a symbol of survival. She fed it and allowed it to fly freely around the apartment; she treated it like a pet. But you didn't know about your aunt's attachment to the fly. As soon as you passed through their door, you saw the fly and swatted it swiftly with your hand. In a second, it was dead. Your Aunt Julča never forgave you.

While this uproar was taking place, your father and I were on our hike. We walked from Jablonec to the Ještěd Mountain. The air tram was already in use although we couldn't afford it, so we climbed on foot. The men walked briskly; I could barely keep pace with them. I tripped crossing the railroad tracks and tore a muscle in my ankle. (Years later, the doctor operated on that ankle, but it still aches from the injury. I have poor blood circulation in that leg, and it always feels cold.) If that wasn't enough, the winds on top of the mountain blew my hat away. I was having my troubles, but not Papa and Janoušek. They climbed down the mountain singing in a jolly mood. Who would think then that your father would be next to die—stricken in the prime of his life like Aunt Julča's beloved fly—and only a few months later?

How the Socialist Party helped during your father's illness

Your father was a member of the Socialist Party. That name is confusing since the Socialist Party of that day was different from what it is today. In your father's time, socialism really was more like what you would consider liberal capitalism today. They were strongly opposed to Communism.

I am so grateful to the Party because they helped your father and even me in so many ways. In his early days at the post office, a Party official used his influence to help Papa switch from being a letter carrier to a package deliveryman, a position that allowed him to earn more money. Instead of delivering letters on foot, he rode with the delivery wagon driver dropping off packages at each stop. His customers almost always tipped him. (Only one man never did; instead he gave Papa a 100 crown bill at Christmas time.)

When he could no longer work because of his illness, the Party arranged, on two separate occasions, to bring Papa to a sanatarium for medical treatment. These treatment centers were high up in the Tatra Mountains of Slovakia. Your father raved about the beauty of the place. The first time when he returned, he looked like he was recovering. He had gained weight and looked healthier, but he soon started to lose weight again.

In the early stages of Papa's illness, the doctors' diagnosis was consumption. Then the doctors discovered that he also had stomach cancer and transferred him to a hospital in Praha for an operation. Uncle Konůpek rented a taxi and took me, you, and your little brother, Mirek to the hospital to visit Papa. It didn't take the doctors long to see he was wasting away, so they let him return home to die. That was the end. Your father died of cancer on January 4, 1934 at age thirty-eight.

Fortunately for me, during that time when Papa was seriously ill, the Party did what was necessary to make sure that Papa was fully vested in his retirement fund. He was only months away from that point, so the party chief felt moved to help out. Because of his caring, I was entitled as Papa's widow to receive his full pension. Otherwise, I wouldn't have received anything at all. After Papa's death, I was directed to go to Praha to get the pension papers processed. I don't know how I found the clerk whose signature was required on the petition form—but I did. I was so frightened. My whole life was in his hands. The clerk saw the recommendation from the Socialist Party chief, looked at me, and signed.

After your father died, I was supposed to return his postman's uniform. Every three years, the postal service routinely issued new uniforms. As it happened, a few months before Papa died, he got a new uniform. Again the Party came to my aid. They managed to get an old uniform for me to turn in to the post office, and I kept Papa's new one. I brought the new uniform to the tailor who cut it down to make it into a coat for Mirek, then five-years-old. It never fit him very well, but at least it kept him warm.

Settling affairs after *tatínek*'s death

Two years later, my own father died at age sixty-seven. *Tatínek* was a heavy pipe smoker, which aggravated his asthma, but he actually died of emphysema. *Tatínek* did backbreaking work all of his life. There is no comparison between the way he lived then with the way Czechs live today.

When *tatínek* died in 1936, we were called to the notary office in Turnov. All of us were present, including my stepmother and her three sons. She managed to have my father leave everything—the house and farmland—to her and my stepbrothers. He left his children only one hundred crowns each. The notary wasn't satisfied with that arrangement and asked us twice if we had any objections. My sisters didn't say anything, but I protested. "None of us received anything when we left home, not even a goose-down comforter." An argument followed. I don't remember much of what was said, but my stepmother had to give us more—two hundred and fifty crowns each. I bought a sewing machine with that money. I still have it.

Chapter 7
Surviving in Spite of It All

Jára's background notes
Before and during World War II: 1936-1945

Pre-World War II was a traumatic time for the Czech people. Although we and our neighbors were glad to have an independent state, all was not well in our country. We were affected by the worldwide economic troubles that became the Great Depression. Many people in Jablonec who had been industrial workers lost their jobs. Land reforms were inadequate, so the farmers in the surrounding areas were also hurting. As the head of a single-parent household, my mother had it tougher, despite her pension, than families where two adults could contribute to the family's sustenance. But in spite of hardships and the ominous pre-war tensions, she managed to maintain an atmosphere of normalcy in our home.

Our family, typical of the times, knew that our first order of business was survival—finding enough food to keep us reasonably nourished. Under the blanket of war, everything else was secondary. Teenagers today may say, "I'm leaving home. I can get my own place." I couldn't possibly think that way. There was a war. Where could I go? I really don't remember if I ever had any heated arguments with my mother, but I realize now that I didn't appreciate her very much or feel gratitude for what she did for the family.

What I was most interested in was bicycling. Mother bought me a bicycle when I was twelve, and this introduced me to a new freedom. Bicycle riding opened up the possibility of exploring a wider environment, something very exciting to me. During the war years, we didn't have enough to eat. Some days I was on my bike many hours riding from one neighboring village to another in search of food. Sometimes I rode alone, but mostly my mother and I traveled together. We went to

Rovensko and Libuň, where our relatives lived, or to various other local destinations. We stopped to talk to farmers, hoping to find those who would sell us homemade bread or some other wholesome food on the black market.

It was okay for families to use the land around their homes to grow a few vegetables for personal consumption, but we were forbidden to raise animals for food. Farmers had to sell whatever they produced to the occupying government. Only food not needed by the German military was made available to the general public through rationing; it was obvious to us that we would go hungry unless we found other means to supplement the meager rationed portions.

Mother grew some vegetables, but our garden was not large enough to sustain us. We had to buy food on the black market, but such dealing was considered sabotage, depriving Germans of food that should go to the soldiers at the front lines. Nonetheless, many people hid chickens and managed to keep a small quantity of eggs for themselves. Occasionally, we could find decent bread at the bakery or grocery store. If we were well acquainted with the owner, he might reach under the counter and take out a special bread for us. We could buy all kinds of things with rations stamps, but only a small quantity of each. For instance, we might be able to buy one egg per week per person with the stamps.

Next to our house in Dalimĕřice was a huge vegetable field privately owned by a large landowner, a former nobleman whose castle was in the neighboring village. This man owned all the land in the immediate vicinity and hired people to manage his many fields and laborers. Nobody tried to buy from this man because we knew he cooperated with the Germans. We knew that he wouldn't allow any of his farm products to be sold on the black market. But we didn't hesitate to help ourselves to some of his potatoes.

When I turned eighteen, I became eligible for cigarette ration stamps. Many Czechs were heavy smokers and craved cigarettes, so my supply of these stamps gave us something valuable to trade for food. In fact, I continued this trade of cigarette stamps for food until well into the Communist era, sustaining our family at a time when providing adequate nourishment was a constant challenge. Unfortunately, Mother couldn't augment our bartering power, since these stamps were issued only to men.

Although Mother was busy with us kids in the years following my father's death, she did find time to have several boyfriends, two of whom are discussed in the next letter from my mother. It was with Josef that she had her longest relationship (Josef is discussed in Chapter 10); but there were also other men interested in her. I was in my preteen years in 1936 when her boyfriend, Fayks, arrived on the scene for his tumultuous six-month stay. This man, whom my mother hardly knew, landed at my mother's doorstep and started directing our lives. He was a religious man and insisted that Mother and we children go to mass every Sunday, even when he didn't. Although he hardly knew me, he didn't hesitate to give me harsh beatings whenever I talked back to him. I don't know why my mother allowed him such latitude. Maybe she thought he was disciplining me for my own good.

In retrospect, I actually do think he really cared about me and wanted to straighten me out. Actually, he accomplished more than he ever imagined. At the time Fayks arrived, I was on a vocational track in my studies. He insisted that I go to gymnasium (eight years), to prepare me for entering university. This change in my schooling was pivotal for my future as a professional. For that I have Fayks to thank. However, the day my mother chased him out of the house, and I saw him walking to the railroad station carrying his suitcase, I was overjoyed. I followed sufficiently behind him so he wouldn't detect me because I had to see with my own eyes that he really was leaving and would be out of my life forever.

Other than Josef and Fayks, Mother had a few other boyfriends, but they never moved in with us. They were farmers in the area. At least one offered to marry her, but she would have had to give up my father's pension if she did. That, she was unwilling to do.

Mother's letters to me only briefly discuss the impact of the Nazi occupation on our lives, but that impact was nonetheless substantial and worthy of some elaboration. What Mother's letters do clearly convey is that, despite the tensions and difficulties of the war years, we managed to live our lives with some degree of normalcy. For instance, toward the end of the war, my brother and I took dancing lessons and attended some dances even though dancing was forbidden. The Germans said, "Our soldiers are on the front, they cannot go dancing, they have to fight, so no dancing here either." Or perhaps their real motive was to prohibit groups of Czechs from congregating together.

Even Mother found time for a few pleasures. She liked hiking, and I remember a few hikes we took together. She also liked to read. We had some books, but we could borrow more from the public library. When my father was alive, he belonged to a subscription book-of-the-month club. That might seem odd, since we had little money, but Czechs considered buying books a necessity, not a luxury. We saw ourselves as a cultured people.[28] I remember being told that the Czechs had the highest literacy and book-ownership rates in Eastern Europe at that time. In any case, we certainly aspired to that title. Even if we were poor, we had books. If not, we were ashamed. Books were considered prized possessions. They were also seen as powerful objects because they carried messages that could inspire or inflame people into action. This perspective was reinforced when our churches and governmental organizations banned and even burned books carrying messages they opposed.

In the middle of the war, Germany announced a policy called *Totality*. This meant that all activities had to contribute toward a German victory.[29] Everything was geared to that end, so we Czechs were stripped of our basic human freedoms. The Germans practiced complete censorship over the press. We couldn't assemble in groups. They monitored all communication.[30] We tried to get correct information from radio broadcasts, so we listened illegally to broadcasts, primarily from London. When the Germans first discovered that we were listening to these broadcasts, they tried to block our reception by putting static noise over the radio signals. Then the Germans issued an order that anyone having a radio must bring it to a special store where they cut out the short-wave band coils (required to receive foreign broadcasts).[31] It was very easy to put them back, which we did, despite the threat of punishment. I remember the small label we had on our radio. It said, "If you are caught listening to foreign broadcasts, you will be sentenced to death." We were not permitted to remove the label.

And we knew the threats were serious. The firing squads did not do their work in public, but the results were widely publicized. It was always announced in the paper—a long list of names. It would say: "The following people were shot yesterday . . . because . . . " and then it would give their names, ages, and where they were from. It went on and on for some time. For lesser crimes, people were sent to concentration camps, and many people died there. The executions escalated after Heydrich, who was the Reichsprotektor of Bohemia and Moravia, was assassinated. My mother mentions this assassination in her letter.

At the time of the assassination, the Germans had our country under complete domination. Any significant Czech resistance came from the outside. In a bold move, Czech partisans in London parachuted down into Praha and killed Heydrich, the highest German ranking SS officer in the Protectorate (Western Czechoslovakia).[32] In retaliation for Heydrich's death, the Nazis began a reign of terror. They executed many people, sometimes hundreds of people in a day. The local newspapers, now under Nazi control, published long lists of names of Czechs executed for such crimes as listening to foreign broadcasts or failing to report the names of guests visiting their home.

I remember two policemen coming to our house one day and showing us some photographs. They asked us if we knew those people. They were suspects in the Heydrich killing. We had to sign a piece of paper swearing that we didn't know them. The policemen threatened us: "If we don't find these people, every tenth Czech will be shot no matter who they are. One, two, three, four, five, six, seven, eight, nine, TEN." Eventually the Germans found those responsible for the assassination and surrounded them. The Czech partisans were hiding in a crypt under a Greek Orthodox Church in Praha. The Germans surrounded the crypt and had orders to flood it, making it impossible for the Czechs to escape. To avoid capture, the partisans shot themselves. But the Nazi's brutal acts of revenge continued. Most notably and horribly, the Germans carried out a massacre in the nearby village of Lidice. Out of 503 Lidice inhabitants, 192 men and seven women were shot and sixty women and eighty-one children (out of 205 women and ninety-six children) died in concentration camps, mostly in the gas chambers.[33] As a final touch, they burned the entire village to the ground.

There were few Jews in our immediate vicinity. I don't remember a single one in Daliměřice. In Turnov, a city of 10,000, there were maybe 100 Jews. These people were rounded up, and they quickly disappeared. Jews and those married to Jews were taken to concentration camps. None were left. It was a tragedy, but most of us Czechs did not realize it or care enough to take much notice. Yes, we saw what was going on—the Germans separating the Czechs from the Jews, making them wear the yellow star of David on the left side of their shirt or jacket to immediately make them visible and distinguishable from the rest of the population—but it was all in the periphery of our vision. For those of us living in small towns like Turnov, the Jews were a tiny minority in the background of our lives. I knew only one Jew personally. He was my classmate. His name was Jan. Often after classes we walked home together. He lived much closer to school than I did. I always walked with him to his house; maybe we stayed outside talking for awhile, then he went inside and I continued walking the rest of the way home. One day, he wasn't in school any more.

I also remember a particular mathematics professor I had who wasn't Jewish, but was still a target of the Germans. When the German army came (I remember the day: the fifteenth of March 1939), he stood in front of our class and said, "What a terrible thing is happening, Germans invading our country. We have to behave like little grasses. We must bend with the wind now, but later, we will stand tall again. If we behave like rigid trees, the storm will knock us down." He told us to be cautious. He saw clearly what was coming. We didn't at that time. We didn't understand what was happening. He told us to be careful, but he didn't take his own advice. One of his students or someone around, hearing him speak in class against the German invasion, must have informed on him because the Germans later arrested him for underground activity and sent him to a concentration camp. He died there. That was the price of failing to bend like little grasses.

During this time, my mother enrolled me in a silversmith trade school in Turnov to protect me from being sent me off to Germany to work in a munitions factory, the fate of those not in school or working. I had almost completed the course of study—three out of four years—when the Germans closed the school. They converted it into a factory that ground silicon crystals for radios. Instead of studying silver-smithing, I was now a factory worker in the same facility. But I was there only three months before I was transferred to another factory in a neighboring city, about twenty kilometers away.

The new factory was a huge place. It was formerly a textile factory, but it was converted by the Germans into an airplane manufacturing plant. The work was totally unsuited for me. Fortunately, the war was coming to an end and, besides that, I had a little accident. I stepped on a nail. It punctured my shoe and the point cut into the bottom of my foot. I left the nail there on purpose. After awhile it started looking pretty bad. I don't know exactly what problem developed with my foot, maybe blood poisoning. When I went to the doctor, he said, "You cannot go to work," and he gave me a permit to stay home. I was elated! I really treasured that wound. The permit gave me some time to rest.

May 7, 1945—that was the day Germany capitulated. The announcement came that Hitler was dead. The war was over. I was twenty years old. I picked up a newspaper and took it with me to the Jizera River to celebrate in my own way. Happy in my heart, I laid down to rest in a meadow by the river. A few minutes later, my tranquility was interrupted by a shot overhead. It seemed to be coming from the German army barracks about three-quarters of a mile away. It took me a moment, but I soon realized that one of those soldiers was shooting at me. He hadn't heard that the war was over, or maybe he simply wasn't ready to give up yet. I began to crawl back rapidly in the direction from where I came and dove into a convenient trench. I heard a second shot and decided to get further away. I climbed carefully out of the trench and, staying as low as I could, crawled along the railroad tracks. As soon as I was a safe distance away, I started to shake, coming to terms with being a sniper's target and with the reality that the war's official end was not necessarily the beginning of paradise.

On the following day, May eighth, it happened again. I was walking with several friends on a country road when the Germans started shooting down at us from a small aircraft. The bullets hit about fifty feet from where we were. We hid behind a huge old tree, and the plane never came back. On May ninth, the Russians came to liberate us.

We were overjoyed to see the Russians. We could not see the dark clouds coming over the horizon; we didn't realize that the Soviets would be our next enemy. We were absorbed in our struggle to start new lives in a new republic. Being twenty, I was able to watch the political wrangling that was going on with some degree of understanding. But like many others, I couldn't foresee what would happen. At least we enjoyed the next three years of relative freedom. Here, Mother describes how those war and post-war years were for her.

Tonča's letter to Jára

It was 1936 when I first met Fayks. He was a charming man, but a big liar. One of his sons in the late 1940s became a big shot in the Communist Party. (I remember seeing the son on television talking about his life.) When I think back now to that time in my life, I am deeply ashamed. I always had less brains than I could use. I started to learn about the world much later, when I began reading good books.

In my innocence, I became prey to Fayks. Even though I was won over by his lies, I didn't completely trust him. In fact, I sent him a telegram telling him not to come, but he didn't receive it in time. He was already on the road on his way to my home when the message arrived. I said nothing about the telegram when he appeared at my door. Since he was already there, I decided to give him a chance to prove himself. I allowed him to move in, and all was peaceful for a while—until I received a polite letter from his son, Květoslav, who knew where I lived from the return address on the telegram. Květoslav wrote that Fayks had been living with him. He said that his father was already married and that he had not been in his right mind since he suffered a blow to the head while he was working as a railroad laborer. Without saying a word, Fayks had left home and was traveling aimlessly on the trains until the railroad canceled his train-riding privileges.

When I read the letter, I threw Fayks out. I gave him a rattan suitcase for his clothing in exchange for his wooden luggage. (That luggage is still in the attic at Klášterní Street.) He filled up his suitcase with a few extras—the linens and towels he stole from the Kos family who lived in the apartment below. This is how I was paid for my misplaced trust and stupidity.

Hitler's advance

One day in 1938, just before Germany took over Sudetenland, I was riding my bicycle through Rádlo on my way to Jablonec. When I arrived at the Jablonec railroad station, I saw German militia in black uniforms collecting money for the war effort. The number of Germans in Czechoslovakia at that time was quite large, about twenty-five per cent of the population. Most of them were pro-Hitler German nationalists. Of these, the majority lived in the borderlands in places like Jablonec.

My friend, Janoušková, and her son and daughter, who were living in Jablonec at that time, fled like many Czechs did in 1938. The family needed a temporary shelter, so I invited them to stay with us for a while. For ten days, Janoušková, Jenda and Líba stayed with us in our crowded apartment. You slept with Mirek, while Janoušková slept with Líba in the kitchen. We pushed our things aside to make sleeping space in the storage room down the hall for Jenda. I was glad to help, but later I was annoyed when my long-time friend didn't offer to give me a single crown to cover expenses; she was content to just sponge off me. When I asked her to pay for her family's milk, she got offended and moved to Mladá Boleslav where her husband was working for the railroads.

In my opinion, it was Janoušková's fault that Jenda died. Jenda had looked sickly for years, even when he was thirteen or fourteen years old, but the family didn't realize he was suffering from consumption. Meanwhile, his mother forced him into a study program, and the demands of it made him even weaker. To get to school on time, he had to wake up at five in the morning and catch an early morning train to Liberec. He became more and more unhappy with his studies and was becoming sicker and sicker. He finally died, five years later.

Jenda's father died in a train crash a year before his son's death. On Christmas day in 1943, Janoušek was on a train riding to the sanatorium to visit his son. Two trains collided, and that was the end of him. After that, his widow found another man. Why? I don't know. During the years she was married, she never wanted to sleep with her husband. They quarreled often. Yet, for some miraculous reason, she and her new boyfriend seemed to get along well. Whenever the two of them felt like having a good meal, they would suddenly appear at our doorstep. I'm not talking about a period of two or three years. This went on for more than thirty years, until I was almost seventy!

Nazis' impact on the schools

Remember, Jára, how you were forced to leave *gymnasium* [high school] in the middle of your studies? The Nazis ordered your school to drop four classes, which amounted to one hundred and twenty-five students. Those youngsters who were allowed to continue their studies qualified based on their high grades in German. That wasn't you. So you were one of the seventy percent expelled from *gymnasium*.

I was concerned about what you should do next. There weren't many choices. You left it up to me to find something for you because the situation was baffling. Openings in higher education were becoming more and more limited. The Germans were regularly closing down colleges, converting them into armament factories.

I saw that you were handy with electrical appliances when I bought a radio and you knew how to pull the wires around the furniture to make the proper connection into the wall. (I realize that it seems silly today to be impressed with the ability to plug in a radio, but I was, being that radios were such a strange thing to me.) I thought that it would be good for you to apprentice with an electrician. In Ohrazenice, there was a small electrical shop. I talked to the owner and arranged a deal with him. But a friend of mine warned me that electrical work was a difficult trade. "Electricians have to climb high up and swallow a lot of dust when they're making openings in brick walls to install wiring," she said. So I decided that you should do something else.

I enrolled you in a trade school. During the winter, when the school had to close down because of a lack of heating coal, I found you a temporary position in an office where you worked as a messenger clerk. You brought home your first salary of one hundred crowns and gave it to me. With this money, I bought you a used world atlas. The atlas cost the entire one hundred crown bill!

It makes me feel good when I think about how I succeeded in keeping you in school. During the war years, you were safest there.

Doing what I needed to do to survive

During World War II, coal was rationed. We never had enough to take us through the cold winters. Fortunately, we had firewood to burn when our coal supply ran out. Oh, how I labored gathering wood! First I would make piles of brushwood in the forest. Then all of it had to be dragged to the road where a horse-drawn wagon could pick it up. I remember once making two piles of wood at the Valdštejn Ruins and then dragging one pile home with me. Afterwards, I returned with a wagon and driver to pick up the second pile, but this left no room for me, so I had to trudge home on foot in the winter cold. Another time, I collected a pile of brushwood from a ravine. I carried the wood up to the road, cut it, and then split it.

I did everything myself. Your father was no longer alive and, silly me, I never thought of asking you for help. Only now I realize that I could have taken a shortcut through the woods or asked you to come meet me with your bicycle to help carry the load. You were fourteen years old then and certainly could have been a big help. It is obvious that most of the time I didn't think clearly, and I paid the price for my mental slowness throughout my entire life.

Gathering firewood wasn't the only heavy job I did. I also did fieldwork for a farmer. I received one hundred kilograms [two hundred and twenty pounds] of grain for one hundred hours of labor. In the fall, I collected leftover potatoes from the ground and carried them home on my back. From farms as far away as Karlovice, I carried large sacks of apples on my bike so you and Mirek would have good fruit to eat. I cut grass with a scythe and then spread it out to dry to feed our rabbits.

Food was scarce; the only way we survived was to trade. Bartering was more valuable than money, which was inflated and almost worthless. Most of what we needed we got through bartering. I remember how you used to save your ration of cigarettes and trade it for food to keep us alive. The government knew that most people smoked and regarded cigarettes as a necessity. But neither of us smoked, and we were happy to trade your cigarette allotment for basic food items.

I used my bike for transportation and for hauling the articles I traded. One time, I rode to the village of Svijany, which was a tiring ride because the last stretch was a steep hill. Over one arm, I carried a coat that I didn't like but which was still in good condition. I met a farmer in the village who was willing to give me sixty kilograms [one hundred and thirty-two pounds] of barley for the coat. Next, I had to get the barley to the mill to have it ground into flour.

The steep climb and my dealings with the farmer were easy compared to getting to the mill with my loaded bicycle. The sky was getting dark as I walked along an abandoned dirt road between the fields. I was leading my bike with the sixty kilograms of barley tied to the seat. I don't know how it happened, but suddenly I was sprawled on the ground in a ditch with my bike on its side next to me. There was no one in sight. I tried to move the weighted-down bicycle back onto the road, but couldn't. I was so frustrated and exhausted I just sat down and cried. Finally, I pulled myself together and managed to get the bike upright and back on the road again. Riding on the level ground wasn't so bad, but the downhill road that led to the mill was another story. I had to balance the load continually so the bike wouldn't fall again. I pressed on the brakes with all my strength and finally coasted to the bottom of the hill. My arms and legs were trembling when I got off the bike, but as usual, my bike served me well.

After a short wait, the miller took my load of barley and gave me a sack of wheat flour in exchange. Then I lugged the flour home with me. I don't remember how much flour I received, but for all I suffered, I deserved every speck I got. On the other hand, I considered myself a lucky woman because the Germans didn't notice me, and I was able to avoid forced labor. Jára, I would have hated to work in a German factory making guns for the Nazis!

Living under German Occupation (1939-1945)

Everything we saw or heard was censored by the Germans. They occupied top positions in all important offices. They ran the post office, railroads, and other transportation centers. That simply was how life was in those days. We had to adjust or go crazy.

The Nazis also controlled the schools and decided which subjects would be offered. They redesigned the course work to increase the number of hours per week of German language study. What's more, they rewrote the textbooks to show history from the Nazi perspective. Do you remember, Jára, when you had to memorize and recite two full pages of the *Life of Adolf Hitler* in German?

The Nazi horror

I was carrying a pie home from the bakery one day when I met a neighbor lady who lived in Halbrštat's house, near the highway. She told me the latest news, a Czech killed Heydrich [in 1942, the Reich protector of the Protectorate of Bohemia and Moravia]. I said, "Good, he deserved it."

"What are you saying? That kind of talk is punishable by death!" she exclaimed. She frightened me, but that was good. If she were someone else, I could have ended up in a concentration camp or dead.

The three of us (you, me and Mirek) were living in Daliměřice at this time. All the news coming from the radio broadcasts was bad, and we were terrified of what might be coming next. We listened to the names of those arrested hoping not to recognize anyone we knew. But we did—the father of one of Mirek's schoolmates. I scanned the newspaper looking for more familiar names at the same time dreading what I might find. More bad news. I noticed the name of my favorite teacher. She was the one whose notes I once delivered to her lover. Sick at heart, I went to bed and wept.

Several years later, at the tail end of the war, I was riding my bicycle from Jičín to Turnov when the Germans came marching through Libuň. They were on their way to Praha, perhaps in hopes of defending one of their last strongholds. There wasn't a living soul around; everyone was hidden, only me on my bicycle riding beside them. I was lucky the soldiers didn't throw me into the ditch running along the road. A friend once asked me, "Weren't you afraid?" I really wasn't. I was so naive.

I didn't find out until later about the gun battle in Libuň that took place soon after I had passed by. When the Germans were advancing on the highway by your uncle's house, two Czech partisans shot at them from the railroad overpass. The soldiers immediately shot back and the partisans dropped. They hit the platform and fell over the edge, tumbling to the ground below. Seeing what happened, the postmaster ran out of the post office into the street. He was probably thinking that he could act as a go-between since he spoke German. The Germans shot him right away and also killed the clerk who ran out after him. Then the soldiers strutted in lockstep through Libuň, firing into the windows of houses along the street.

Your cousins, the Cardas, happened to be visiting your Aunt Anča and Uncle Jaroslav in Libuň that day. Everyone in the house rushed to hide twenty-year-old Pepa under a pile of potatoes; afterwards they hid themselves as best as they could in various spots around the house. They knew it was crucial that the Germans not find Pepa. The Nazis considered young men of fighting age a military threat. Fortunately, the Germans didn't try to enter anyone's home. The war was coming to an end, and the Germans were focused on getting to Praha. If it weren't for the challenge by the partisans, the Germans might have marched straight through. And think of it, unsuspecting me innocently pedaling along on the road next to the retreating Nazis.

Chapter 8
My Neighbors in Dalimĕřice

Jára's background notes
Pre-war and World War II: 1934-1945

Mother's letter briefly describes what life was like for her and her two school-age sons in Dalimĕřice. Mainly, she concentrates on her neighbors in a series of quick sketches that give a flavor of typical daily life in communities throughout northern Bohemia. Since we were out of the borderlands (we used the Czech word, *pohraničí*; the German term, *Sudetenland*, was distasteful to us) everyone was Czech, which meant that there were no more ethnic struggles. Dalimĕřice was one of the small communities that sprung up outside the city of Turnov. It was not an independent township. It was simply a housing tract and considered part of the greater Turnov area, but it had its own mayor. Our house, adjacent to farmland, was in front of a military drill field where, every morning, we'd see soldiers from the Czech army marching by our house.

Although Dalimĕřice was a housing development, it was not like the ones we are familiar with today. The houses did not look alike because they were built by different builders. A family would buy a lot and then arrange for the construction of a house, either by a professional builder or by family members and neighbors.

We moved to Dalimĕřice because it was a cheap place to live. My mother rented an apartment in a private home, and we shared the bathing and toilet facilities with our landlord. We had to live very economically since my father's pension was our only income. However, this seemed like adequate space to us; living three to a room was a common practice. We were glad to find these living quarters, and our landlord was equally happy; his family depended on this added income to survive.

This, too, was common, since most Czechs we knew could not afford the luxury of a private home without boarders.

In Dalimĕřice, like in most small communities throughout Czechoslovakia at that time, we knew practically everyone. Generally, we were all from the same area since people usually stayed put. If somebody did move, usually for job-related reasons, it was within the same region, and he or she usually maintained ties to the hometown or village. In our community of Dalimĕřice, there was very little cultural diversity since we shared the same history and language. Even with our peculiarities, we were more similar than different. Certainly, we didn't always like each other. But at worst there was a kind of a reluctant relationship because of our common roots and experiences. So our neighbors and their families were a big part of my life. These relationships meant even more to my mother, a widow with two children. The community served the function of an extended family for her. Of course, she wouldn't have expressed herself in that manner. If anyone would have asked her what she needed for herself and her family she would have answered, "Food, a place to live, and something to wear." Yet, as described in Mother's letter, we were an extended family with all the warmth one would expect—as well as the pettiness.

Tonča's letter to Jára

After your father's death in 1934, we moved to Dalimĕřice where living was cheaper. Since it wasn't far from Rovensko, I rode my bicycle back home to see my father and stepmother frequently while *tatínek* was alive. You must have many childhood memories of the community of Dalimĕřice, Jára, because you and Mirek grew up there. I have vivid memories of my own. There were no paved roads yet or even gravel pathways. Oh, what mud! I couldn't keep up with the shoe cleaning. After a rain, the streets turned into a giant hog wallow.

The apartment that we rented from the Vitásek family had enough space for the three of us to live comfortably. We had a large kitchen, a bedroom, and a storage room. The indoor toilet and wash room we shared with the landlord's family.

We bathed and scrubbed our clothes in the wash room [laundry room] where there was a wooden tub and a stove that could burn either coal or wood. On laundry day, I dragged the tub to a spot close to the floor drain. Then I heated up water on the stove. After filling the tub with hot water and dirty clothes, I took a big bar of laundry soap and rubbed each piece of clothing, one at a time, against the corrugated steel scrub board. Whenever I wanted to change the water, I pulled the plug on the bottom of the tub, and the water came pouring out onto the floor and down the drain. How lucky we were at that time to have such luxuries! (In our next home, the toilet and wash room were outside.)

When we first moved into our home, the owner lived on the first floor. Then Vitásek got a good job in Slovakia and moved there with his family to be near his work. When they moved out, the Kos family moved in. For several years, Vitásek was our absentee landlord—until things in Slovakia worsened. Many Slovaks didn't like Czechs, but the government had kept the situation in check. With Slovakia's new status as an independent puppet state under the Germans, the Slovaks were able to do as they wished—to clear out as many Czechs as possible. That's why Vitásek lost his job in 1939 and had to return to Dalimĕřice.

Although our place was on the second floor (not where the Vitáseks used to live), we still had to vacate our flat. That's because the Vitáseks preferred to have the Kos family, rather than us, as tenants. They had an employed father and so seemed more stable compared to us, an unemployed widow with two young children. So we moved out and the Kos family stayed.

The neighbors

Although many of the incidents that happened to my neighbors didn't involve me directly, I felt like they did, because these people were an important part of my daily life. That's why I remember them so clearly.

When we were forced out of our apartment, we found another place, further up the block. Vitásek was no longer our landlord, but he still was one of our neighbors. After the war, his small strawberry patch became very successful and he was able to buy more fields. Vitásek was the first person in the area to start a strawberry business. By 1960, he was known as the Strawberry King. His daughter, Dorota, married into a rich family. She had two children, but her husband divorced her. Maybe his parents didn't like her and broke up the marriage. Or maybe his family was snobbish and didn't think the Vitáseks were classy enough for them.

Dorota and her children moved back home with her parents. At about the same time, her younger sister, Radka, married a doctor and began building a lovely villa near the hospital in Turnov. They never had any children, but ended up adopting Dorota's two girls to give them a strong, two-parent family. It seemed like the best solution all the way around, especially when Dorota's ex-husband's family threatened to take action in court to obtain custody of the children.

Another neighbor, the Skořepas, built a house on an empty lot close by. I used to see their little daughter playing in front of their house on sunny days. The husband was still a young man when he died suddenly in bed. He didn't appear for breakfast at his usual time, so his wife went to wake him up. She found him already cold and dead.

Behind the Vitáseks there was a house where the Tesařs lived. The Tesařs had a son, Jirka, and a younger daughter, Eliška. It was on one of those dreary fall afternoons that four-year-old Eliška wandered over to a plowed, water-soaked field to play. The clay earth was saturated by the heavy autumn rains. Eliška, unaware of the danger, stepped into the deep mud and couldn't pull herself out. If I hadn't heard her crying and come to her rescue, she could have sunk in pretty deep. The sky was already turning dark, making it hard for me to see her from my window. I ran out of the house straight to the spot where Eliška was stuck and yanked her out of the mire; one of her shoes stayed behind.

Across the street from us lived the Bíleks. They rented their apartment on the first floor from Pepina, who owned the property and lived in one room on the second floor. The Bíleks had two children, an older girl, Marie, who died when she was twelve of some mysterious illness, and a younger boy, Tomáš, who was in poor health. After the war, the Bíleks bought a very small cottage with a huge garden from a neighbor down the road. They tore the cottage down and build a house on the lot with two apartments, one for themselves and the other for Tomáš, who married eventually.

Pepina and her sister, Hrobařová (who lived next door), were both very religious. In 1938, Pepina married a man she met through an advertisement in the Catholic newspaper. I walked by her house on the day of her wedding and saw her sitting on the doorstep crying. "What's the matter, Pepina?" I asked.

"I just found out that the man who is coming to marry me is much older than he said," she moaned.

Well, she married him anyway. What else could she do? Unhappily, Pepina sold her house and moved with her husband to the mountains of Českomoravská Vysočina. There they lived in a small cottage isolated from all other human contact.

Next in line was Láska's house. Láska was an old man, but he lived with a woman much younger than he. Her daughter, about seventeen at that time, also lived with them. No one knew about the girl's father; her mother didn't have a husband when the child was born. A man named Kuchař also lived with them for awhile. It didn't take him long to seduce the daughter, but at least he was honorable and married her. They had five children together.

Next was the Kratochvíl's house. They had a daughter, Věra, who was still a child. (Věra later married poorly, into a life of constant toil.) I met Kratochvílová on the street once when she was walking home from work. "I want to die," she told me. And she did within a month. She wasn't sick. One day, she went to work and was fine until the moment before she died.

Her husband didn't remarry, although the widow, Vitáková, proposed to him. She was a fat, unattractive middle-aged woman with doubtful marriage prospects for the future. She thought, *I am alone; he is alone. Maybe we can join together.* Kratochvíl didn't think so.

The Kupka family lived in that same house, but in later years. The wife died young and left her husband with a two-year-old child. As many widowers did, especially with small children, he remarried quickly, in my opinion, too quickly. Instead of providing his son with a good home, he gave the child a stepmother who hated and abused him. The little boy suffered a lot, especially when Vlastík, his stepbrother, was born. When Kupka's son was four or five, his grandmother finally took him away and raised him in Ohrazenice. If only it had been sooner. When he grew up, he entered the military. One afternoon, another soldier found his body—he had shot himself dead.

In 1939, we moved into the Halbrštat house, number eighty-nine. Our neighbors across the street were the Urbans. The father was a violin teacher. Once he stopped in to see me and offered to give violin lessons to you or Mirek. Where would I get the money? I was paying for bicycles on installments and for other things that were more important than violin lessons. The Urbans had a daughter, Lída. Do you remember her? She married a butcher and had twin daughters on Christmas day. They had a house near the railroad station and were fairly well-to-do. For some reason, Lída soon got a divorce. How could she have afforded to do that? What was she thinking? I've had to scrimp to make your papa's pension cover basic expenses, and here she was married to a rich man, and she divorced him. I could understand it if he beat her, but he didn't. He wasn't impotent. But, what do I know? Only Lída can say, and it's too late now.

Zučenko, a Russian-born immigrant, lived on the street in back of us. When the Russian soldiers came into Czechoslovakia in 1945, Zučenko was afraid that they would capture him and kill him, so he went into hiding. His wife went looking everywhere for him. She finally found him and brought him back home. The Russians left him alone. Another Russian, who lived with the Urbans family, wasn't so lucky. When the Russians came, they took him away immediately, and no one has ever seen him since.

These Russian neighbors were fugitives from their homeland. They ran away, but not far enough. In 1945, after the end of WWII, the Red Army remained in Czechoslovakia for about a year. They said they were there to protect us until we could set up our own government. Our Republic was still in its infancy, not in any position to challenge a strong country like Russia. How could we block them from removing Russian runaways from Czech soil? Whenever the Russians received a tip that one of their countrymen was hiding in a Czech household, the soldiers came and searched that home. If they found someone hiding there, he was handcuffed and sent off to Russia as a criminal. To be fair, during that first year, the Russian soldiers rarely interfered in the lives of Czechs in our community, just Russians.

Across from the grocery store and three houses down stood the Villa Krása. A plaque with the word "Krása" [beauty] hung outside near the entrance, and the villa lived up to its name for a while. It had a well cared for rose garden plus other flowers decorating the front of the house. But Berka (I will tell you more about him later [in Chapter 10]) bought the place in 1950. His wife was a poor housekeeper and when he died in 1970, her careless ways carried over to the garden as well. She brought in two dogs to guard the house and, between their damage and her neglect, the garden grew into a wild tangle.

Across the street from the Villa Krása lived Aunt Valentová, who was related to us somehow. I'm sure you remember her. Her husband at one time (1939) was manager of the brewery in Hrubý Rohozec, and they lived right there on the premises. Too bad Berka's wife didn't have Aunt Valentova manage the Villa Krása gardens. She had a way with plants and animals but had no opportunity to use that talent at the brewery.

The Kordík family built their own home sometime after 1945. It took a long time to construct because they did all the work themselves. They didn't have children of their own, but they adopted a little girl named Hedvika, who for some reason, developed a hunchback. In spite of it, she married. Her husband was an inmate from the Institute for the Physically Handicapped in Liberec. When they got married in 1960, he left the Institute, and they set up housekeeping. Although they were both handicapped, they were able to help one another, and they were happy together.

On the back street, I only knew the Toušek family. The husband, a cranky little man, was always looking for something to complain about. He certainly didn't hesitate to make trouble for me. He had the nerve to report me to the authorities because I had some rabbits in a hutch that I was raising for food to help keep our family alive. You know how scarce food was during wartime! Because I didn't have a vegetable garden, he figured that I must be stealing plants from someone else's garden to feed the rabbits. (At that time, no one would have paid good money for vegetables just to feed their rabbits.)

The truth was I used to go to the edge of town where there were open fields left unattended by absentee landowners. I would pick the broad-leafed weeds and bring them back to my rabbits. A policeman came to investigate the complaint Toušek made about me. When he saw that I had only five rabbits, he left. Nothing came of the incident. And what happened to Toušek? He was shot dead by the Germans during the last days of the war. The Russians were going from village to village liberating us from the Germans, but it wasn't soon enough to save Toušek.

Other Dalimĕřice townspeople

The mayor of the village held a responsible position in the post office. Official Nazi arrest reports addressed to the Gestapo in Jičín passed through his hands. The mayor made it a practice to destroy those documents and, by his actions, saved the lives of many innocent people. When his wife died, he moved out of his house and told his children it was now theirs. In the early 1950s, he moved in with the widow, Votrubcová. He was the third and final widower to live with her.

Although most of the residents of Dalimĕřice lived with their families, some elderly folks shared apartments for companionship and to save on costs. Others, such as widows and widowers, lived alone while they were hunting for suitable new partners. There were also a few folks who lived on the fringe of society, yet they still were considered a part of the overall community. Jára, you probably remember the two beggars, Vašíček and Kačaba. Once I was walking behind them on the back road that led to the railroad station. Vašíček was scolding Kačaba, and every so often Vašíček gave his friend a push that landed him on his backside. Kačaba jumped up playfully, and I had to laugh. During a terribly cold winter, I heard that they both froze to death while asleep in a pile of straw.

On the second floor of the house where we lived, we knew an elderly couple named Červinková and Procházka. Červinková was content begging for a living as long as each day she earned enough to buy Procházka a small bottle of rum. He was lazy and depended on her to take care of his needs.

Červinková's and Procházka's apartment was infected with fleas and bugs. One day, our neighbor, Bĕlohlávek, got mad about the situation. He threw their furniture into the backyard and burned their straw mattresses. Grabbing a paintbrush, he covered the grimy walls of their one-room apartment with a coat of white paint. His wife and I painstakingly plucked out the bugs from the furniture with tweezers and threw the insects into a jar of alcohol to show our landlady. (She didn't believe that the old couple had bugs all over their apartment.) We washed the furniture: a bed, a small table, two chairs, and a piece of luggage, and made everything tidy. After all our hard work, the old couple, instead of being grateful, cursed us.

In 1945, when Červinková was unable to walk anymore, she had to go into the nursing home in Sychrov. Procházka then moved into the building where the butcher Číhal had his shop. By that time, I had already moved to Liberec, but I bumped into the old fellow again when I returned to Dalimeřice to visit a long-time friend. Procházka, dressed quite decently, was walking leisurely in front of his house smoking a cigarette. "I have a small pension," he explained, quite self-contentedly.

The widow, Maryšková, lived upstairs above a cabinetmaker's shop, in the last house on the main highway running through Dalimeřice. I could write a book about her, but I don't want to go into all that. She was always nice to me and our family, so why would I want to tell unkind stories about her? She was really a good person, full of fun and mischief. People liked her because of that, but there were those whom she offended. She was always flirting with men even when she wasn't trying to. It was just her way. Remember, Jára, when she teased you as a young boy? You and she were walking together past a ladies' shop when she stopped and pointed to a bra in the window. "Jára, do you know what that is?" she asked playfully. I will only say that I visited her in Valdice at Jičín, where she bought a nice house. I hardly recognized her with all the weight she gained.

Another landmark, the Ouhrabka villa, was past Číhal's butcher shop on the highway between Dalimeřice and Turnov. When my sister, Máňa, was fifteen years old, she was a servant at that villa. At the time, it was owned by the Chief of Police. Máňa couldn't stand the stress of all the work required to keep up that big house. It wasn't only the cleaning and family laundry. She also had to take care of the house guests who constantly came and went. So she quit and walked out. The police chief's wife got mad and sent a policeman to our house to make trouble for our family. I was only three years old then, but I remember his uniform, a helmet with long rooster feathers. We saw him coming down the path to our house, and we met him at the door. We let him in when he told us that he had an order to search for linen; the police chief's wife claimed she was missing a bedspread. We had only one small dresser. The policeman peaked in there and left. (Shortly afterwards, he died in the big explosion in the Rovensko Town Square. He was the same policeman who lit his cigar near the cauldron of gas.)

As I was growing up, I gradually came to know the police chief and his wife. This was because she had a sister who worked in the pharmacy in Rovensko. In summertime, the wife used to come to visit her sister in a fancy horse-drawn carriage; in winter she drove up in a covered horse-drawn sled. I never liked her. I used to say to myself, "What a stuck-up witch!"

Chapter 9
In-laws and Other Assorted Vermin

Jára's background notes
1922-1972

A major source of aggravation for my mother came from within her family. In my mother's community, people's lives centered around the immediate and extended family. They provided friendship and support, but with this closeness came irritation as well. In my mother's case, she had to contend with a variety of relatives, the most irksome being her brothers-in-law, that is, her sisters' husbands.

My mother's letters, filled with stories about serious illnesses, show how vulnerable we all were to the diseases of the day. For example, *consumption* is a term that often appears in my mother's letters. As is well-known to readers of Dostoevsky and other writers of the time, it was the old term for tuberculosis, but I didn't realize how old that name was until I looked it up and found that the disease has been known since ancient times when it was widespread and usually fatal.[34] Sadly, these facts hadn't changed much since the days of Hippocrates, at least not in Czechoslovakia in the early part of the twentieth century. Tuberculosis (TB) wiped out most of my close relatives. It was impossible to avoid exposure to the disease. Everyone I knew either died from it, or had it at one time and fought if off successfully. I myself was never aware of having had TB, but my X-rays show evidence of past infection.[35] TB hit people of all ages, but the weak or sickly were the most vulnerable, as were the malnourished—a category that included the majority of us.

Poor nutrition was also a contributing factor to the high infant mortality rate. Mothers, as is true today, had to leave their infants in the care of others when they went to work. But unlike the present, there were no infant formulas, and the poor could not afford wet nurses. Babies were often just given a wet cloth to suck. These cloths were generally dipped in a concoction that was so weak or unwholesome that babies died of malnourishment, diarrhea, or some infection that they couldn't fight off in their debilitated state. More fortunate babies were given a cloth soaked in a gruel made from semolina wheat that was mashed and combined with water or goat's milk.[36] This is what my mother refers to when she mentions feeding infants semolina mash.

As noted earlier, the state of medicine was, in retrospect at least, dismal. Health care was minimal. Mother's letter briefly discusses visits by friends and relatives to spas (mineral hot springs), which were a key part of what passed for the health care system. Individual spas specialized in the treatment of particular ailments. These spas have had a long cultural tradition in the history of Czechoslovakia. Some of the famous spas, such as Mariánské Lázně (Marienbad) and Karlovy Vary (Karlsbad), date back to the fourteenth century. Another spa, at Teplice, had its origin in the twelfth century.[37]

In some cultures, people rely on prayer to cure the sick. I would not make that claim for Bohemia. Although Czechoslovakia was considered a Catholic country, for most of us, our Catholic affiliation was more a label than a religion (as was discussed in chapter three). As hinted at by Mother, we thought anyone who was devout was peculiar, one of the eccentrics in our midst. However, in eastern Czechoslovakia, religious attitudes were different. In the Moravian region, or the Silesian region near the Polish border, the people's roots were more Slavic than ours, and they were genuinely Catholic in their beliefs and practices.[38]

Although Czechs tended to be secular, they maintained the custom of celebrating their *name day,* the day associated with the name of their patron saint.[39] In many European countries a name's day remains more important than a birthday. My mother talks about observance of her name's day, but not her birthday.

In this letter, Mother covers a large expanse of time. For instance, she returns to the tensions that were starting to build in Bohemia near the German border, an area that had developed into a German overflow zone. During Mother's earlier years, there was a comfortable "live and let live" relationship between Czechs and Germans. But this attitude faded rapidly as the twentieth century progressed. During the World War II era, Germans in the borderlands (or *Sudetenland,* as they called it) spoke only German and sent their children to separate German-speaking schools.[40] They considered themselves Germans; on that point we agreed.

In Bohemia, at that time, people were identified by their ethnicity (such as German, Polish, or Hungarian), not by their country of birth. (This is still true today.) Ethnic groups rarely assimilated.[41] They lived in their own enclaves and kept apart from the general Czech population. Despite the linguistic and physical separation between ethnic Czechs and Germans, some young people in Jablonec managed to find each other, intermarry and have families. My Uncle Emil, who my mother discusses in her letter, was an example. He was the product of a household that was strongly German even though his father was Czech. Emil's father's second marriage, that occurred when Emil was a small child, was to a German woman who brought him up in the German culture. Although Emil chose to remain in the area during World War II, his reasons for staying were not political or philosophical. He stayed because it was convenient. Emil was an opportunist who did what was easiest or most profitable in any given situation. Living as a German in the borderlands (that we Czechs called *pohraničí*), during the war, clearly gave him more opportunities than living as a Czech in the interior of the country that was then the Reich Protectorate.

In contrast, Emil's brother-in-law Oskar was a true German (on both sides of his family), even though he too was born in Czechoslovakia. As Mother mentions, he and his wife owned a restaurant before the war. But it was nearly impossible for most inns to stay in business. No one was around to manage them, food was scarce, and the average person couldn't afford to eat out, so there were few customers. Therefore, like so many others during the war, Oskar's restaurant closed.

This was how life was in the Czech borderlands. Czechs ran eastward, away from Hitler's stronghold.[42] Most who stayed were German Czechs like Oskar and people like Emil, who were thoroughly assimilated into the German culture.[43]

Tonča's letter to Jára

As children, we used to visit Mladějov where *tatínek* was born (in 1866). After my grandfather died, my grandmother soon married again. She had two daughters with her new husband, Malát. My grandmother died when my father was five.

Aunts and uncles

One of my aunts later settled in Řepov at Mladá Boleslav. Do you remember when we visited auntie and spent the night in her spare room? We found out later that her guests seldom stayed in that room. That became obvious when darkness came and hundreds of mice crawled all over us in our beds. You managed to ignore them and sleep well through the night, but I was pushing those critters off me until dawn. What a night! Sleeping with mice brought to life my worst nightmare.

My father's other half-sister visited my mother often. On one occasion, she brought our family a big, deep hat with a wide brim. We used it to dry mushrooms in. I remember her well because she was my favorite aunt. When it was time for auntie to return home, I always accompanied her for part of the way. We walked together along the railroad tracks, the shortest route by foot between towns. We preferred to walk, even though there were trains running between Turnov and Jičín. My aunt came to a tragic end. She died while she was trying to save a goose from being crushed by an automobile. Cars were then a novelty, and poor auntie had no idea of the danger of reaching under a moving car's wheels.

It doesn't make sense to compare losses, to say that one family suffered more or less than another, but in sheer numbers of deaths, it's true that your father's family did worse. Jára, all of your father's brothers and sisters died from consumption. Six died young; only one brother and one sister survived until adulthood. I saw a photograph of that brother in military uniform. I don't know when he died; perhaps it was during military service. The sister married someone from either Most or Duchcov. I don't know how many children she had, but I met one of her daughters once at a funeral. My mother-in-law survived all of her nine children and passed away in 1934.

My mother-in-law's marriage to Masák, the forest ranger

It was 1924, and I had just been married. I stepped off the train at Hradiště Station and started my hike to the ranger station where my mother-in-law lived. About halfway there, I saw her coming along the dirt road carrying a sack of butter. She was on her way to the market in Hradiště. My mother-in-law at that time was married to Masák, her second husband, who worked as a forest ranger. Her first husband was a roofer. He was killed when he fell off a roof during one of his typical drunken stupors. He left behind his widow and nine children. Jaroslav, your father, was the youngest.

Mother (as I called her) was close to fifty when she accepted a job as Masák's housekeeper. At the time, his youngest daughter was still living at home at the ranger station. After awhile, Masák and Mother got married. She was happy with him despite all the hard work she had to do. She enjoyed living in the forest.

Later, one of Masák's married daughters accidently burned her own house down. She had fallen asleep with a lit cigarette still burning. Although she survived, she was badly burned and suffered brain damage from all the smoke she inhaled. Her husband drank too many beers the night before and couldn't wake up in time to run out of the burning house. Their young son was, for all practical purposes, left an orphan. My mother-in-law sized up the situation and brought the boy home to live with her and Masák. She raised him until he was a young man, as if he were her own son.

Life at the ranger station

There was no running water at the ranger station. Mother had to carry the water she needed up the hill and through the woods in a big wooden pail strapped to her back. Whenever I stayed with them, I helped carry water, too. Mother could have had a water pump if her husband had seen some value in making life a little easier for his wife. When his employer (the nobleman who owned the castle and the surrounding land) offered him a lump sum of money or a water pump, he took the money and let his wife continue to lug the heavy water container on her back. Once a year, the nobleman gave Masák a pail of firewood to use for household fuel. He always sold it. As a result, Mother had to continue collecting firewood from the forest to burn for the family's needs. It was also Mother's responsibility to care for a cow, pig, and chickens. Of course, she had to carry in water for them, too.

Stupid me! During my summer vacation when you were a baby, I picked you up from your foster parents in Rovensko and took you with me to the ranger station. It was during the harvest season, so I helped in the field. I put you on the ground while I was working. We had potatoes for lunch and potatoes for dinner. The ranger didn't eat potatoes with us. He wasn't hungry because he filled up on smoked meat while Mother and I slaved in the field. Mother wanted to fry us some eggs, but her miserly husband wouldn't allow that. I still didn't learn my lesson, because the next year I returned, this time to help out on Masák's daughter's field. (By then, the ranger was retired and Mother and he were living in his son Karel's inn.)

Masák only cared about his own five children. He didn't like me or my sisters, and he made it obvious whenever we visited, which wasn't often. He expected his children to kiss his hand, even after they were grown. As a daughter-in-law, I didn't know I was also supposed to. For *his* children, it wasn't a bad deal, since he gave each of them 30,000 crowns when they reached adulthood. In contrast, Mother saved during her whole lifetime and was able to put away only 5,000 crowns. She gave all of it to Papa and me for a wedding present.

My brothers-in-law

To tell you the truth, all of my sisters' husbands were worthless. František was impotent when he married Růža, and Jaroslav was a women chaser. Emil wasn't a bad fellow, but he didn't like to work or put himself out for his wife, Julča. Of the four brothers-in-law, Konůpek was the most despicable. Poor Máňa!

Máňa's husband, Josef Konůpek

In the days when we were still both single, Máňa and I visited a fair in Smržovka where I ate my first banana. Máňa bought it for me, and it was a very special treat. Since bananas weren't a local fruit that we could pick off the trees, they were unknown to me except in pictures. How sweet the banana tasted with a softness more like pudding than fruit.

Máňa, by that time, was already dating Konůpek who was also at the fair, but as a vendor, not a customer. He was there to sell his shoes. The shoes he had for sale were handmade, but not custom made. He kept them in stock ready to sell as needed at fairs and open-air markets everywhere. In 1922, Konůpek was working for Novák the shoemaker, the same man who later hired me as a maid.

From the time she was fourteen, Máňa worked as a maid for well-to-do families. She married Konůpek when she was twenty-eight. Before Máňa met Konůpek, she dated a baker for six years. Just before the war [WW I] broke out, he and Máňa made plans to set up a shop and take an apartment together. They never did because he was among the first to be called to duty. My sister mailed him packages all through those war years. He survived and returned, but not to marry Máňa. He didn't even come to see her. He married someone else in Náchod, his hometown.

Máňa was getting older and marriage opportunities were becoming scarce when the villain Konůpek showed up. My sister got pregnant early on in their relationship. When she saw his brutal nature, she decided to leave him. He responded by threatening her with legal action if she had an abortion. She felt trapped into marrying him. A few days after their wedding, she ran away with the intention of leaving him. But she didn't know Konůpek!

At that time, I was a maid at the Janovský's. From the hallway, I could hear yelling and then the doorbell ringing. I answered the door and Konůpek leaned toward me and shouted, "I am going to fix it so your husband is fired from the post office!" He hollered several obscenities and ran back into the darkness.

I didn't know it then, but I found out later that Papa had brought Máňa's luggage to her at her girlfriend's apartment in Rychnov where she was in hiding. Konůpek searched all day with no success, then at night he finally found her at her girlfriend's place. It was already dark outside. Máňa and her girlfriend wouldn't let him in, so he ran around and around the building causing a ruckus cursing in Czech and German until Máňa gave in and left the house with him.

Jára, you probably didn't know that Máňa gave birth to two daughters. Her first was born in a cottage in Lochov next to Prachovské Rocks where there was only one nurse for several villages. The infant wouldn't nurse from Máňa's breast, so they tried Konůpek's mother's idea, having the baby suck on bread soaked in water. The baby didn't survive. She died of an intestinal infection. (My mother didn't breast feed me either, but she gave me semolina mash which was healthier. Semolina was a common food to give babies then because mothers couldn't leave the fields or factories to nurse their babies. Of course, there was no packaged infant formula, and even if there were, who could have afforded it?)

Later, Máňa and Konůpek found an apartment in Jablonec. They had a second daughter, but unfortunately this one came to a sad end too. She was born with blisters all over her body. In six weeks, all of them disappeared except for one on top of her head. Then that blister burst and she died. What caused her death? Nobody knew. Babies were born, babies died. It was just the way it was in those days.

My brother-in-law, Konůpek, was a crazy shoemaker if ever there was one. He lost 5,000 crowns gambling, and that was big money then. He also drank a lot. In his later years, he needed full time supervision because he was so wild and unpredictable. Once his nephew, who was supposed to be looking after him, left him alone locked up in his apartment. When he returned, he caught Konůpek just before he was about to escape through a second story window by lowering himself to the street on bed sheets tied together.

I don't know what words to use to tell you how much I hated Konůpek. He was just plain nasty! I can't forget how he spoiled my name's day when I was twenty-seven years old. Your father gave me a special present, a necklace with glittering little garnet stones. I thoroughly enjoyed being the center of attention that day. When Konůpek arrived, we all got ready to go out together for a walk. Suddenly Konůpek saw the new necklace on the table and shouted, "Who gave Tonča such a luxury?" In one swift move, he grabbed the necklace and flung it against the table where it broke into tiny pieces. The family didn't know how to deal with Konůpek, so they kept quiet. I was sad and mad at him at the same time. On our walk to Vrkoslavice, there was an ice cream stand on the roadway. Konůpek bought your little brother an ice-cream cone, maybe as a way to apologize to me. But your uncle's gesture did nothing to heal my feelings and caused Mirek more pain than pleasure. He became sick with bronchitis a couple of days after eating the ice cream. I still get angry, Jára, whenever I think back on that incident.

Konůpek always gorged himself whenever Máňa made goose for dinner. On one of those occasions, his meal ended with an attack of bad cramps and diarrhea. He jumped up from the table and ran out the door into the night. He continued running through the streets until he came to the railroad tracks. Lucky for that bastard no train came by. He squatted down where the nettles grew, and all that happened was the prickly plant burned his bottom.

My sister had a dreadful time with him. Her life was a nightmare. He was mean, stingy, and had a furious temper. She was constantly afraid of what he might do next. Everywhere they lived, he quarreled with the neighbors. During those thirteen years they lived together, they moved seven times. He couldn't get along with anybody.

When Papa and I moved into our new apartment, Konůpek decided that he wanted to sleep there overnight and arrived at our door with Máňa. No one got any sleep except Konůpek. All night long, we heard the nauseating throat-clearing sounds of him bringing up spit. He was a heavy smoker, and his windpipe was ruined from years of smoking. We suffered with him for one night. Poor Máňa had to hear those sounds every night! Death was a real liberation for Máňa.

Máňa told me, "If I die before you, everything that I have will be yours." But when she died in 1936 from tetanus, I didn't receive even a handkerchief. At that time, Máňa and Konůpek had about 50,000 crowns. I never received anything because Konůpek tampered with some documents to make it look like he had outstanding loans in order not to give us sisters any inheritance. We didn't even brood over it. We figured that Konůpek would do this sort of thing. He used the money to buy large quantities of leather for his shoe business. (I have to admit he made good shoes and was very prosperous.)

Shortly before she went to the hospital, Máňa washed the laundry and hung it in the attic to dry. Believe it or not, somebody stole it. Konůpek, the idiot, accused me of stealing it. I didn't even know what their attic looked like, not to mention the fact that I lived in Dalimĕřice, twenty-five kilometers away. He was carrying on, accusing me of theft during the time when we were all mourning Máňa's passing. Well, what could you expect from such a heartless man so unfeeling and miserly? I will never forget how when Máňa bought a T-shirt for Mirek, Konůpek scolded her like she had done a terrible thing. Despite the fact that he liked Mirek and that Mirek visited his aunt and uncle often, Konůpek never gave Mirek anything (unless you count the ice-cream cone).

After Máňa's death, Konůpek used to visit the cemetery and cry at her burial place. One night, he got drunk and left his false teeth on her grave. In the morning, he couldn't remember where he had left them.

Then he got the idea that he wanted to court me, being that I was a young widow. He promised me a cottage and a cow. Suddenly there was money! When I refused him, he made a terrible scene. Soon after, in 1939, he remarried, this time to a German woman.

During the war, somebody reported to the police that Konůpek was listening to foreign radio broadcasts. He was thrown in prison and would have remained there much longer than he did if it were not for the aid of his new German wife. Konůpek didn't even own a radio, but he probably had said something, maybe boasting to his drinking buddies. He was beaten in prison and, when he was finally released, he came home from Litoměřice on foot, full of lice. His money, along with anything else he had in his pockets, was gone.

I was glad that he suffered in prison. He and his family were trash. They were always suing each other or their neighbors over inheritance or property rights. Everyone else avoided the courts like the plague, but Konůpek and his family were quite willing to go to court if there was any chance of grabbing money for themselves. Because their claims were below a certain minimum, they could go to a type of court where lawyers weren't required. They could never have afforded to sue if they had to pay lawyers.

Julča's husband, Emil Kovář

Emil's mother died when he was young, and his father, a Czech shoemaker, remarried to a German woman. All of the children in the family attended the ancestry-based German school. Emil grew up thinking of himself as German. Emil, had a brother, Rudi, and two sisters, Anna and Roza (more about Roza later). Anna lost her mind after the war [WW II]. She wandered through the streets unaware of where she was or where she was going. She soon died in the Kosmonosy [mental hospital].

The brother, Rudi, lived in Liberec in one large room. Like Konůpek, he was a shoemaker by trade, so he used his room for a workshop as well as a place to sleep. He married late in life to a Polish woman of questionable character. She moved in with him, and one month later they got married. When baby Eva was born, the family wondered about the speedy wedding and doubted whether Rudi was actually Eva's father. Rudi died a short time later, after the birth of their second child, a son. His wife died of cancer when Eva was five and their son was three. The children ended up in an orphanage. A couple from Praha adopted the boy, but Eva stayed in that orphanage until she was grown. Julča had wanted to adopt her. She didn't because Emil was against it.

For as long as I can remember, Julča never liked village work. Once, while I was helping at the threshing machine, I saw her approaching with a little bundle over her shoulder. She had just quit her job at the mill after working there only two months. To improve her chances of getting a better job, she moved to Jablonec to learn German. Afterwards, she spent two years in Bratislava, where she had gone in order to recover from a disastrous love affair. I remember that she then brought her next boyfriend, a railroad employee, back to Rovensko to meet our family. But when he saw how poor we were, he didn't want to marry her anymore.

Julča had a short relationship (exactly one month) with a man named Straka. Soon after they broke up, he married a very fat lady who used to sell frankfurters near the dam. You children used to call her Mrs. Frankfurter. Straka loved this woman very much. I can't imagine why! He had to dress her, tie her apron, and lace her shoes. When she died in Turnov, he bought her a marble gravestone, not new, but exceptionally nice. On the first Christmas after her death, he went to the cemetery and set up a Christmas tree next to the gravestone. He decorated the tree with his wife's favorite candies and some special holiday sweets in the shape of candles. Throughout the night, Straka sat beside her grave keeping watch on the circle of lighted candles he had placed carefully around the Christmas tree. When morning came, a cemetery caretaker found him still in a trance, mourning the passing of his beloved wife.

Julča first met her husband, Emil, when she was nineteen and he was twenty-five, but they didn't get married until ten years later. Too bad they didn't wait another ten years and then forget about the idea. I say this because Julča's marriage was never happy. Emil should have married the German girl he had a child with when he was still single. Instead he abandoned them to their fate. The child died a few years later.

When I first met Emil, he was delivering bread in Jablonec, although he was a confectioner by trade. He had gone all the way to Dresden for training, but he never put his knowledge to use.

Emil was a lazy fellow. From the very beginning of his marriage to Julča, he did what he wanted when he wanted and did nothing at all when that was to his liking. He took off every Sunday afternoon to watch skittle in winter and football in summer. He took advantage of Julča, who was too sweet-tempered for her own good. Emil retired at age sixty and after that didn't lift a finger to contribute to the household.

In the early years of their marriage, Emil and Julča lived by the forest on the rim of the city. She had to walk up and down steep hills to get to her place of employment. In winter, it was always a struggle for her to keep her balance on the slippery, icy ground. Julča suffered a bad fall one evening, coming home from work and spent three days in the hospital with a concussion.

Later, Emil and Julča found an apartment above the railroad station. Their lease was for an apartment on the third floor, but a couple living on the ground floor level grabbed the vacant third floor apartment the moment it became available. Julča was happy to get away from the forest and didn't notice the switch right away. Neither did Emil. That wasn't surprising; he never paid any attention to anything except his personal comfort. He left all worries and household affairs to Julča.

Living on the ground floor, they were constantly bothered by passers-by muddying up the area in front of their apartment. Tenants trudged by with their dirty shoes, often lugging threadbare sacks of coal from the cellar to their apartments. Just like the other tenants, Emil and Julča had a small windowless space in the cellar for storing coal for heating and cooking. They carried the coal from the street down the dark stairs to their storage area. That was always a miserable job.

Julča and Emil had a child many years into their marriage. It hurt Julča to see Emil attentive to other kids yet show no feelings for their own son, Rudi. When Emil came home from work, he ignored Rudi. Their son wasn't allowed to speak or make any noise in his father's presence. To Emil, it was more important to read the paper undisturbed than to take any interest in his little boy.

I don't understand why you children and many others seemed to like Emil. Julča was particularly upset about his popularity. When it became obvious how heartless Emil really was, none of my sisters liked Emil anymore. In fact, Růža made it clear that she didn't want her brother-in-law to be buried in the family plot. (He was buried there despite our wishes. His nephew managed to sneak it by us, after his uncle begged him on his death bed in Kosmonosy.)

I remember the time when Julča, working at home making costume jewelry, couldn't find one of the stones she was working with. She looked desperately for it, almost losing her mind. Weeks later, she was in Jičín and saw that jewel on Líba, Emil's niece, and knew at once who had taken it.

He even stole money. Julča had to keep her money hidden from him. I don't know how she could carry on through so much aggravation. Růža and I had to hide our valuables from him, too.

There's no doubt, Julča had more bad than good with Emil. He gave her only sixty crowns per week, which was very little. He didn't eat at home; he preferred to have his meals at his sister's inn, where he was working as a waiter. When Rudi was a two-year-old, Julča had to take on housecleaning jobs to earn some extra income. The stingy allowance Emil gave her did not cover even their most meager basic household expenses.

Rudi died when he was five years old. The exact cause of his illness was never really clear. As was customary at that time, the doctor hardly told Julča and Emil anything about what was wrong. He didn't explain the course of the illness or give them any information about what to expect. But it was obvious from Julča's letters that Rudi was terribly ill. Since the doctor could offer no treatment or cure, Julča turned to an old folk remedy. She made her little boy drink kerosine. He died soon after. When we heard the news, I decided to take you and your brother to Jablonec to attend the funeral. (We were living in Daliměřice at that time.) Although we usually couldn't cross over the border from the Protectorate to *pohraničí*, we told the German guard that we wanted to attend a family funeral, and he let us pass.

Before the war, Emil worked at an inn owned by his sister and brother-in-law, Roza and Oskar. The only other employees were two waiters and a cleaning lady. Roza and her husband paid Emil a salary that was very small, considering his responsibilities. Oskar could easily have afforded to pay more.

The waiters stole from the business and Emil knew it. In fact, Emil also helped himself to money from the cash register. His measly salary wasn't enough to support his strong craving for cigarettes. Our family was able to excuse his dishonesty, but what we never forgave him for was the way he treated Julča—his never giving her any help or consideration.

When most Czechs were fleeing Jablonec, before Germany annexed the borderlands, Emil decided to stay with his family and blend into the German community. He was ordered to report for road repair work, but Roza interfered. She talked her brother into accepting a post with the German military police. His fluency in German no doubt helped him get the position.

Emil's first job in the military was to guard Czech prisoners. There were three buildings behind the railroad tracks near Vápenka in Liberec that were used for prisoners. It was Emil's job to walk the prisoners to wherever they were needed for the particular work project of the day. Sometimes relatives came by with packages of food for the men. Emil received some packages too. He was helpful, always pointing out where the relatives would find the prisoners they were looking for. In the beginning, the job was fairly pleasant, but as the war progressed, Emil was sent to guard the bridges. That responsibility was a lot more dangerous than he bargained for. I don't know all the places he went, but I do know that he never was sent to the front. The last time he came to Libuň, he was dressed in German uniform. Our family told him never to wear that hateful uniform again in front of us.

After the war, Emil spent time in a prison camp somewhere in Brno. When the Russians liberated Czechoslovakia, they sent Emil to prison because during the war he had worked for the German military police. Julča visited him there and told us that almost all the prisoners had swollen arms and legs. Emil, being the kind of person he was, made friends with the camp leader, and so he didn't suffer too much during his stay in prison.

Life returned to normal, which for Emil meant indulging himself once again. He was a heavy smoker. To be nice, I used to bring him Lípy cigarettes. One day, he told me, "You know, Toni, I don't smoke Lípy any more; I smoke Startky." Startky cost two crowns more; he took pleasure in asking me to bring him the more expensive cigarettes.

But that was a small thing compared to the way he treated my sister. Emil knew that his smoking was uncomfortable for Julča, who suffered from several serious illnesses. It was obvious he didn't care. He even had the gall to send her out on brigades, the public service work program that I will tell you more about later. But, of course, Emil never went himself.

I'll never forget that when Julča was lying in bed dying, Emil said to me, "I didn't marry her to be waiting on her hand and foot." He didn't take any interest in Julča's welfare when she was in reasonably good health. In her weakened, invalid state, he completely turned his back on her.

Oskar wasn't a scoundrel like his brother-in-law, Emil, but he had a weak character. Roza and Oskar opened their inn during the First Republic, a time of great economic opportunity in Czechoslovakia. The restaurant was a gold mine, but they mismanaged the place. One thing, however, Oskar did do well. Every morning he arrived well-dressed and made his rounds, stopping at the tables to chat pleasantly with his guests. Roza, on the other hand, was never there. She spent her time traveling from spa to spa or traipsing off to Italy. Eventually, they lost their inn because they were terrible managers. They immediately rented another restaurant behind a dam on a small peninsula next to a swimming area. Of course, the war changed everything. Oskar, being German, was arrested at the end of the war and sent to a prison camp; Julča and I visited him there. Later, he was transferred to Germany.

After the war, Oskar (now divorced from Roza) remarried, this time to a woman he met in Germany. A short time later he divorced her too, which was strange because divorce was uncommon in those days. He then set himself up in business operating a food kiosk and made a lot of money. It's not surprising he did well given his familiarity with the restaurant business. Julča brought Roza over to visit me once after the war. When I saw Roza, I knew she was suffering from starvation. A short time later, I heard she died from eating spoiled sausages.

Those two waiters who used to work for Oskar—they also died, one then the other. They were still quite young, somewhere in their thirties. Their graves were next to each other. Julča and I noticed them when we visited the grave where Rudi was buried.

Růža's husband, František Benda

When I first met Růža's husband, František, he was living with his brother's family in Jičín. His brother was a businessman who owned a beautiful villa in Ořechovka, the nicest part of Jičín.

František was a moody kind of person with a gruff way of speaking. Maybe he was crabby because of his impotence. To my surprise, I found when I got to know him better that he was an intelligent man. He was particularly knowledgeable about Czech history. František became interested in talking to me when he found out I also knew a bit about that subject.

Růža's sister-in-law (František's older sister) outlived Růža, whom she wore out with her constant demands. The old woman spent several years in a nursing home located about three train stations beyond Jičín. Růža visited her often. She would write to Růža, "Bring me some medicine from the drugstore." František's sister had a pension, but never thought of paying Růža for the cost of her train ticket. Instead, she took advantage of Růža's kindness.

It was that very same sister that urged Růža and František to adopt Líba. Růža and František had been married about fifteen years with no children when they heard about Líba. Adopting a child was a nice thing for them to do; I can't say anything against it. František's sister lived somewhere near Líba's parents at the time and knew they were looking frantically for a good family to take their baby. Líba's mother was anxious to make arrangements for her daughter's adoption before she died. She wanted the peace of mind of knowing that her child would be getting into a good family. Líba was fourteen months old when she came to live with Růža and František. She had both a brother and a father, but the father was willing to give her up for adoption because he didn't want to be burdened with her.

When Líba was still a small child, Růža used to take her to the cemetery and explain, "Here is where your natural mother is buried; I am your adopted mother."

Everything would have been all right if not for Líba's grandmother. She lived nearby and caused Růža much aggravation. This grandmother was a strong, independent woman of fifty-years-old woman, still in her prime. She liked to travel and had no desire to spend her time raising a child. She was financially comfortable with the pension she received and the extra money she earned at home making artificial flowers. When Růža needed her to baby-sit, she had to pay her. But when Líba grew up a bit, suddenly her grandmother started to take an interest in her. Eventually, Líba became more attached to her grandmother than to her adoptive parents. Růža was so hurt by Líba's preference that František forbid the grandmother to visit their home. But it was too late; the bond between Líba and her grandmother was too strong to break. Růža was always yearning for love; she didn't find it in her marriage or with her adopted child, Líba. Her husband died of cancer at age sixty.

František had an elder brother who was a widower. When he became old, he went to live with his married daughter. Unfortunately, she treated the old man badly. He lived like a prisoner. He couldn't go anywhere because she refused to give him a key to the house. He had his own room where he stayed for long periods of time with no one to talk to or help him. He liked beer, but his daughter wouldn't buy him any. When Růža sent Josef (more about him later) to bring some of her homemade pastries to the old man, Josef would stop on the way to buy him beer. Josef handed the beer and pastries to him secretly through an open window when no one else was at home.

Anča and Jaroslav Tůma

Before Jaroslav married Anča, he had a girlfriend in the neighboring village. When he broke up with her, she and her mother ambushed him in the woods when he was delivering mail and beat him with sticks. Jaroslav brought them to court and was awarded 5,000 crowns. The reason why he collected so much was because he was a mail carrier, which was a government position. Anyone who worked for the government was treated with great respect in the community at that time.

Anča's mother-in-law didn't want her son to ever marry. She particularly detested Anča and spoke harshly against the marriage. I don't know if she even knew, at first, that my sister was already pregnant. Nevertheless, after they were married, she moved in with her son and daughter-in-law and lived in their home for twenty years. She slept in her own room. This meant she had half the house because the cottage only had two rooms. She hated her young daughter-in-law so intensely that she refused to say her name. But when the old woman became ill, suddenly she began to call out *"Anča"* and even *"Aninka"* [the diminutive form, used to show affection] whenever she needed her. Anča took care of her mother-in-law until the old woman's death. Her own daughter, Volšičková, lived next door, but she never visited her elderly mother.

Jaroslav hardly gave Anča enough money to survive. My sister had to work long hours in the field for other farmers to make ends meet. During the war, Jaroslav was sleeping with a woman whose husband was away working in Germany. (This unfortunate husband was one of many Czechs forced to move there to work in a factory, replacing the German men fighting at the front.) The husband returned home unexpectedly one day and found his wife occupied with Jaroslav. The man chased him with a stick all the way from his village to Jaroslav's home in Libuň. Later, Jaroslav kept an affair going in Liberec with two women at the same time. After a while, both of those women threw him out.

The Tůmas' children and their families

Anča and Jaroslav Tůma had two daughters, your cousins, Miluška and Bóža. When Bóža grew up, she married Pepa Carda and had three children.

Bóža and Pepa had a happy marriage, the only one I knew of. They always loved each other and still do today. After what they suffered beforehand, they really deserved their happiness. From the start, Anča and Jaroslav were against their daughter's marriage and tried to block it. They applied even more pressure when Bóža's sister, Miluška, died during childbirth. Anča and Jaroslav wanted to be sure that Miluška's infant had a good mother, so they tried to force Bóža to marry Béďa, her sister's widower. But Bóža wanted to marry Pepa. To take care of this problem, Bóža saw to it that Pepa made her pregnant. Then her parents had to accept that she and Pepa would marry and that Miluška's widower would have to find another mother for baby Radek. In the meantime, Radek stayed with his grandparents, Anča and Jaroslav.

The widower remarried some time later to a sloppy woman and careless homemaker. Little Radek, now of school age, went to live with his father and new stepmother. One day his Aunt Volšičková visited them and noticed that Radek's hair was full of lice. It was obvious that Radek wasn't getting adequate care, so she brought him back to Libuň to live with Anča and Jaroslav again. When Radek grew up, he married and settled down in Železný Brod.

Anča was always a strongly religious Catholic, but her husband, toward the end of his life, became a fanatic. For many years, Jaroslav used to travel east to the distant Moravian-Silesian border to see the Virgin Mary and drink the holy water at the shrine.

Jaroslav's side of the family

Jaroslav had one brother and two sisters. It was one of them who married and became Volšičková. She and her husband moved next door to Anča and Jaroslav, who were then living in a house in Libuň. Their place was next to the well where neighbors came for their water supply. It was convenient to have the well nearby, but the comings and goings of the women with their continuous chatter annoyed the two families, especially the men.

Jaroslav's other sister married and became Mařáková. The couple settled in Turnov where they bought a big house next to a school that taught jewelry-making. The two businesses that the husband and wife started, a coal warehouse and a horse wagon transportation business, did well and brought them a lot of money. But they didn't have much success with their daughter, Aninka. The Mařáks were distracted by the demands of their two businesses, leaving them little time for their child. That's why Aninka was raised so poorly with no guidance or direction. Her parents eased their conscience by giving her large amounts of spending money, but what she wanted most was affection. Aninka solved the problem by trading money for affection. As we all knew, her shopping sprees, when she became a young woman, included buying lovers. The guilt money from her parents gave Aninka the opportunity to pay men for their services as traveling companions and lovers.

Aninka had a reputation for wild spending and running up large debts. She drained her parents' finances by her overspending and constant demands for pocket money, and she even cheated them whenever she could. Once I received a bill from Mařáková for coal that I had already bought and paid for at her warehouse. Aninka was working there that day and had obviously taken the money for herself. I took my receipt and went to see her mother about it. I told her, "This is the receipt I got from Aninka when I gave her the money for the coal. I thought you should know." Mařáková pressed her lips together tightly and didn't say anything. I knew what that daughter was like. Later, Aninka married and had two children, then abandoned them to run off to the Krkonoše Mountains to work as a waitress.

Uncle Jaroslav's brother had a daughter who caused him much grief. She had a baby with a man she planned to marry. But the man broke off their engagement when he found out that her parents had financial troubles. Later on, she found a good husband. She didn't appreciate the fellow and was always making fun of him. One day, she found him drowned in the bathtub. The police suspected her boyfriend, but they couldn't prove anything.

Lucky me

I used to wonder why our family has had such poor luck. Yet when I compare myself to my sisters, I can see that, thanks to your father, who left me a pension, I had a much easier life. If not for that, I would have had to work and also take care of two small children. (Before the pension came through, I had to take a job as a cleaning lady at the post office for 300 crowns a month.) Perhaps, there really is something to what my mother said about me being special because I was born on Easter Sunday! You were born on a Tuesday at eight in the morning, and Mirek on Friday at three o'clock in the afternoon. You inherited your father's cleverness; Mirek got his sickly condition.

Chapter 10
My Life with Josef Mužák

Jára's background notes
Post World War II, then the Communist Era: 1945-1984

My mother's letter discusses her later years with her often-drunken boyfriend, Josef. From today's frame of reference, especially in the United States, we tend to view chronic drunkenness as a disease or a disorder, something that needs remedying or curing. That was not true in Czechoslovakia. Heavy drinking was not looked upon as an illness or social problem. It was our way of numbing ourselves to find temporary relief from our frustrations and paucity of choices. Boredom, as much as anything else, was our easy explanation for drinking. And so we thought it was natural for men to drink and smoke. It was expected; it was part of being a man. Women did not have the same privilege. Our double standard did not sanction drinking and smoking for women, who did not necessarily like these habits in men, yet generally accepted them as normal.

As my mother's letters suggest, her life with Josef played out during a period of instability when the country was trying to adjust to the challenges of post-war social, political, and economic tensions.

After the war was over, the Czech people were eager to remove the German presence from their country. As Mother's letter briefly mentions, one of the first things they did was order all Germans to leave. These were traumatic times for ethnic Germans who had lived for generations in borderland cities such as Liberec and Jablonec. But, of course, there was much bad feeling toward anyone of German ancestry, so they had to go.[44] They each were allowed to take twenty-five kilograms (fifty-five pounds) of possessions with them. Grabbing what time would allow, they abandoned their homes and joined groups of other Germans being herded on to trains to take them across the border into Germany.

Sorting out Germans and Czechs was not easy. Due to intermarriage, families often were composed of people from both ethnic groups, so it was sometimes unclear as to who must leave and who could stay. These questions compounded the heartache of severing family ties and the problems associated with relocation.

The houses that they vacated did not stay empty for long. Now free for the taking, these properties were a bonanza for the Czechs who arrived first to stake their claims.[15]

Although my family did not benefit from this property exchange, we were nonetheless elated that the war was over. Unfortunately, we enjoyed only a short period of democracy after the war and were barely recovering from the food shortages and other legacies of the German occupation and war years, when the Communists took over our country in 1948. Again we were robbed of our freedoms and our self-determination. Fear pervaded our lives, at times heightening to moments of terror. Our heavy industry and commerce were put under state control and our agriculture was collectivized. The economy, weak to begin with, plummeted.

Under communism, the state was the only entity that could employ. Capitalism, which included ownership of businesses and related property, was forbidden. The only significant form of private ownership allowed was of our personal residence, but only as long as that residence was not an apartment house with rentals. A home owner could only rent out a single room in a one-family home, as can be seen in my mother's letter. Such earnings produced too puny a profit for the government to fuss about.

People in all levels of society were searching for work or ways to supplement their meager incomes. The problem wasn't only the hardship of job shortages and low pay. Many professionals in the public eye found themselves unable to work at their craft because of ideological reasons. Even established, respected writers were not immune to this problem. The Czech writer, Ivan Klíma, dramatized this situation in his book, *My Merry Mornings.* His fictional characters included writers who were no longer publishable because of communist government censorship. One character says, "My former Chief Editor, a literary critic by training, has for seven years now been employed washing shop windows . . . . The theater director who dared to put on my last play (last of those that could be staged, that is) is serving a prison sentence; apparently, he committed the crime of sending some scripts abroad."[45] Job seekers in all levels of society grabbed on to any business opportunity that came their way, such as selling fresh carp on the street or working as a hospital orderly. Others earned a little working as construction laborers or pilfering goods from their employers for future resale. Klíma writes about how petty theft became institutionalized in a society characterized by poverty, hopelessness and state ownership of businesses.[46]

I had a colleague, a friend, in the school where I was teaching in Moravská Třebová, who felt as I did about communism. We were looking forward to the time when communism in Czechoslovakia would be over. "Next year," we would say, then next year came and nothing happened. So again we would say, "Next year."

But the end never came. With our hope gone, sadly we each had to face the question, "How shall I live under communism? What shall I do?" We each chose a different path. I chose higher education and worked hard to get my credentials. With those, I moved to Praha and got a better teaching position. Then later, in 1969, I left the country. That was my way.

My friend chose another way. He joined the Communist Party and took advantage of all the privileges the Party offered him. I was angry at him when he joined, but later on I forgave him. It was his way of handling a difficult situation.

During this period, I was struggling with a failing marriage. It was then that I became acquainted with my present wife, Blanka. Her marriage was also coming to an end. She and I got to know each other at a summer camp where her daughter, Milena, and my daughter, Alena, were both campers. Blanka and I were married about a year later, in September of 1964. Sometime in the next couple of years, we started to talk about escaping to another country. We continued talking about it until July of 1969, when we actually made the move.

I recall that when I first brought up the subject of emigration, Blanka's response was, "No. I have my whole life here. I don't even want to think about it." Then came the Dubček era, bringing with it restored hope. In the early sixties, a loosening of the firm grip of the Communist regime had started. Even the top Communists realized that reform was needed. Some of the men who tried to make these changes in Czechoslovakia were executed, but the trend toward reform continued. In the late sixties, Alexandr Dubček emerged as the first secretary of the Communist Party in Czechoslovakia. He, unlike many other Communist leaders in the country at that time, was an intellectual as well as a politician. His slogan was *Socialism with a Human Face*. He criticized many practices of the Communist regime and proclaimed a new socialism. He immediately started to implement his ideas, and they caught on rapidly. Freedom of speech, the right to legal justice, and the right to travel freely were quickly reinstated. Uncensored newspapers, books, radio, T.V., and movies were able to reach people. Writers, publishers and producers no longer had to worry about reprisals. He ordered the release of political prisoners and initiated contacts with our Western neighbors. The nation was excited. We anticipated the restoration of full democracy. We were caught up in an euphoria; most of us never considered that these new-found freedoms would not endure. *The Prague Spring,* as it was called, was a fitting name for this time of renewal. Unfortunately it only lasted eight months.[47]

Václav Havel, in his book, *Disturbing the Peace*, explains what precipitated the Prague Spring and why it was smothered so fast. He argues that political and social pressures had built up over time. The party reformers in leadership positions responded by lifting the lid a little to avoid an explosion. But then the Kremlin got scared. They slammed the lid back on the pot before the notion of political plurality bubbling on the surface boiled over the top.[48]

It was the summer of 1968, and Blanka and I were vacationing with our children, Milena and Alena, in a campground near the Bouzov Castle in Moravia. On August 21 st, we woke up to a gorgeous morning. Within minutes after sitting down at our portable table for breakfast, a forest ranger and campground attendant walked hurriedly toward us. He said, "The Russians invaded our country and are occupying Praha."

Over the following days, we felt the reality of living through an invasion. Russian soldiers were everywhere, and we heard sporadic shooting throughout the city. Normal life came to a halt. The Czechs' vigorous passive resistance made use of all available communications to spread ideas and information: newspapers, television (our one channel), telephones (not widespread but useful), and especially the radio.[49] Students demonstrated and sometimes they were shot at, but they didn't stop. The mood had changed; anticommunism now was pervasive throughout the country among all social classes.

Word traveled fast and before long, we were all wearing black ribbons on our lapels as a sign of national grief. A strategy we used to confuse and disorient the advancing Russian units was to remove all street and directional signs and not volunteer any information when soldiers asked for help. We also planned for an hour of noise. One day, exactly at noon, we arranged for all the church bells in the city to ring and the cars in the streets to accompany them with honking horns. The Russians soldiers looked scared; they didn't know what was going on. To unnerve them further, we shouted, "Go home Ivans (what we called Russians), Natasha expects you home." Blanka and I climbed to the roof of our apartment building to get a good view of what was happening in the city. We saw the soldiers running back and forth, turning abruptly, not sure what to do.

The radio station employees barricaded themselves in the building near the National Museum, and we were able to hear uncensored news for a while. During this unstable time, Communist rule was weak, but this did not last long. In a couple of days, the Russian soldiers stormed the building and, once again we heard the hated Communist propaganda: "The Red Army has come to liberate you from a counterrevolution which is threatening to stop your progress toward socialism."

It became clear to us that the Russian soldiers actually believed that their mission was to rescue us from a counterrevolution. Many Czechs who knew Russian talked to the soldiers to explain that this was not true. Before long, the soldiers could see that for themselves; if the Czechs were of one mind, how could there be a counterrevolution? Our effectiveness in deflecting their loyalty was probably the reason why Moscow soon replaced the whole occupying military force with another one.

I think the Russian soldiers succumbed so easily to *our* propaganda because these men were not well-trained, well-indoctrinated soldiers. They were people with minimal education from the rural Caucasus of Central Russia. Many of them didn't even speak or read Russian; they only spoke the language of their region. But the Soviets made sure that the replacement army was better trained than the previous one. Just to be sure, the soldiers were forbidden from talking with Czech people. In fact, after they completed their mission in Praha, the soldiers were moved out to remote military bases throughout our Republic; we rarely saw them again. The Soviet soldiers lived on those bases for over twenty years with their families, isolated from the rest of Czechoslovakia. They were kept on Czech soil just in case of an uprising.

Dubček and other political intellectuals and professors who had been responsible for initiating, encouraging, or carrying out reforms were the main targets of Soviet retribution. Their careers were crushed, and they suffered severe humiliation.[50] Elementary and high school teachers who had been vocal in their support for the reforms during the Prague Spring were persecuted also.

With the end of the Dubček era, our hopes were dashed. We knew that a dark future lay before us. All the privileges we had newly gained from the liberation of Prague Spring gradually were being taken from us, one after another. Fortunately, it was a slow erosion. The border remained open until fifteen months after the Soviet invasion; it was dangerous but still possible to leave the country. Despite the hazards, many people were emigrating to foreign lands. Eventually, our family was among them. Not my mother, sadly. It would be too risky and disruptive for her.

Tonča's letter to Jára

It was early in 1945 when Vitáková, Josef's sister, first introduced me to Josef. Before that, I knew him only by sight. I had seen him shortly before the war started when we were all living in Daliměřice. Our landlord's family had just returned from Slovakia and wanted our apartment, so we had to move out. I found us living quarters in the Halbrštat's home. Josef had a room in the house next door to us at Viták's place, although he wasn't living there at the time. He'd been drafted to work as a laborer in Germany. Like most Czechs, he had to support the German war machine.

There was a massive air raid near the end of the war, which Josef used to his advantage. He escaped during the confusion and found his way to Ohrazenice, where he knew a farmer who was willing to hide him. The family gave him woman's clothing and a scarf to cover his head, which is how he was dressed when he was out in the fields harvesting potatoes. Josef couldn't go home; he knew the Germans would search for him there. After a while, though, they lost interest in looking for him. Besides, the Germans didn't have a system for keeping track of their foreign laborers. That air raid left many dead, and no one cared about what happened to Josef.

Eventually, Josef ventured out of hiding in the evenings to play the accordion for dinner guests at local restaurants. His playing was very amateurish. He didn't know how to read notes, but he had a good ear for music and learned by listening. He also played the accordion at the inn in Dolánky where the Germans used to go. They applauded him, especially when he played "Lili Marlen."

After the war was over, many Czechs rushed to the borderlands to take possession of the homes that the Germans were forced to abandon when they were ordered to leave the country. Their departure left few people available in Daliměřice to tend the fields. Bednářová (one of the village women) would pound a drum to call anyone who was available to bring in the crops. Vitáková and I had to go out to the fields. It was our duty because we were among the few not employed elsewhere. So off we went with a small hoe to work the beet fields without pay, just for dry bread and black coffee.

As we worked, we chatted back and forth. "My brother, Josef, is interested in you. Why don't you and I go to Liberec where Josef is working at the railroad station," said Vitáková. I thought, this is going to be good for me. So I went with her to meet him.

I always envied women with husbands who worked for the railroad because there were special advantages connected with that kind of work. Those families had free train tickets and a supply of coal. Still, I barely knew Josef Mužák at that time. I didn't know then that he was a bit simple-minded and sometimes wild and unpredictable. Josef was the youngest of five children. Their father was an alcoholic who beat his wife. When the Vitáks married, Josef's sister took her mother with her. Old man Mužák, died alone somewhere near Louny.

When the war was over in 1945, you, Mirek, and I were sharing an apartment in Daliměřice. You may remember that we were again pushed out of our flat, this time by another tenant. She wanted our apartment for her daughter who had just gotten married. The couple needed a place to live, so the mother offered our landlord 150 crowns per month. Since we were paying only 100, our landlord told us to match the offer or move out. We couldn't afford to stay, but we had no place to go. Josef heard about our problem and suggested that we all take an apartment together in Liberec. So that's what we did—except for you. You were twenty then and decided to remain in Turnov.

That first apartment with Josef, near Vápenka, was on an upper floor with no elevator and too many steps to climb. I had a torn ligament in my foot, and climbing made the injury worse. The pain became intolerable. I ended up going to the hospital for surgery. As luck would have it, the lady in the bed next to me was very sympathetic. After I told her about my situation, she kindly offered me two ground floor rooms in her villa. We moved in and remained there for two years. In the meantime, Josef left his job at the railroad station. He worked in a warehouse for awhile. Then he took a job as a bricklayer at a silk mill in Rochlice, repairing a wall and building an add-on. While Josef was working at this site, the government sent him a voucher for a fourteen-day all-expense-paid vacation for two at a mountain spa at a place called Velká Úpa in the Krkonoše region. Josef had his group leader to thank for this gift. His leader was well-connected with the labor union and used his influence to see that Josef got rewarded for his hard work.

Let me tell you more about Josef. For a long time, he got around on his bicycle, peddling from one village to another. Before that time, he owned a horse which he grazed near an animal control "shelter." A shelter it was not! I'm not going to write any more about that.

Later, he bought a small motorbike, a Pionýr, and learned to ride it in an exercise field. I was astounded when he passed the driver's exam. He lost that motorbike somewhere outside of Jičín. He was returning home from the pub drunk, zigzagging from curb to curb, when a policeman saw him and took his bike and driver's license away. Josef had to travel the rest of the way on foot. It was a long, long way.

I don't know what to say next. Maybe I should talk about Josef's foolishness and how he paid for it? Once he traded an accordion for a motorcycle. It was a huge motorcycle. Josef could never control that bike. We didn't have a place to put it, so we parked it in our living-room. I told him, "That bike is smelling up our whole apartment." When he finally decided to sell it, nobody wanted to buy it. Finally, someone bought it for spare parts.

Then Josef started an accordion business. That lasted until one particular customer came to our door and said that he wanted to buy an accordion. Josef showed him the three he had recently purchased. It turned out that the man was an undercover policeman, and he hauled Josef off to the police station with the three accordions. I didn't sleep all night long. Josef returned home in the morning without the accordions. When they called him in for additional questioning, I went with him. Josef was so frightened of the police he would have admitted committing even murder. Although not a murderer, he did commit a crime—owning a private business, as small as it was. In spite of the penalties, people started such businesses all the time. Josef was hardly unusual in trying to get away with such things.

Josef lost a lot of money in business, but (with my help) he kept starting over. Perhaps the most unusual business started with a ride we took to visit Josef's friends in Louny. They worked as independent contractors for Collectible Materials, a government-owned warehouse. They had developed a business in recyclables, which means they collected animal skins and feathers. Josef believed that he could get rich doing this business, since those materials were in heavy demand in the clothing industry. He liked the idea so much that he quit his bricklaying job and started to collect animal skins and feathers. And where did we keep this collection? In our yard, of course. A variety of vermin, living on those skins and feathers, moved in with us. We had cockroaches, mice, even wood-boring insects! With those especially, we had a big problem. Neighbors also complained about hordes of moths swarming around our yard.

The landlord hated having that animal stuff around and reported Josef to the Labor Office for not working at his bricklayer trade. The Communists regulated jobs by preventing people from switching from one trade to another. In this way, the government controlled the number of workers for each trade. At that time, bricklayers were in short supply.

A man from the Labor Office came to see Josef and told him he needed a written excuse from his doctor to change trades. The way the system worked was that when you chose your first trade or occupation, all you had to do was register yourself with the government. But to change occupations, you had to get government approval. Being that Josef once was operated on for a hernia, it wasn't difficult for him to obtain a letter from his doctor certifying that he was unable to do work requiring heavy lifting. The Labor Office never bothered him again.

Soon afterwards, we bought a house to get away from troublesome landlords who never could get used to skins, feathers, and vermin. We were lucky because we bought just before the devaluation of 1953. We paid 32,000 crowns and had so little money left after purchasing the house that we didn't lose much in the devaluation. Our only loss was a few thousand crowns, the money that Josef had hidden in luggage and hadn't told me about.

Processing those skins and feathers wasn't easy. Every skin had four legs, each of which had to be supported by a skewer. We then put the whole skin on a V-shaped stretcher. We had hundreds of these! Most of the work came in spring when there were many baby goats. We dried the skins in the garden, like laundry on a line. In the fall, during the hunting season, we processed rabbit skins and resold them to the Collectible Material's warehouse. The warehouse also paid me and Josef to sort and pack these recyclables so that they would be in proper condition to dry and store well.

But Collectible Material wasn't Josef's only customer. He had no trouble finding several good black-market outlets for his recyclables, such as clothing manufacturers and dressmakers. He also found places where he could make money selling his services as a skinner. He put up one of his stands in front of a fish and rabbit market serving customers buying rabbits for dinner.

While working in his black-market activities, Josef met other people looking for business opportunities. I remember a young man who owned a car, which he wanted to use in developing a secondary income. He wanted to work as a collector, too, so he asked Josef to introduce him to a manager of Collectible Material. He also asked Josef to sell him some skins to help him get started. Josef agreed. The next day, the three of us set out on our shopping trip. The man drove us to the tiny port of Hřensko at the German border. Then he waited in the car for us to take a boat up the Elbe River to Děčín, where we bought the skins and feathers we needed. For me, it was a lovely day. I enjoyed the car and boat travel very much, and the young man was happy with the help Josef provided.

People liked Josef. He knew how to handle them. He treated everyone as if they were part of his own family. Because of this, when there was a food shortage, Josef was able to bring home eggs and sometimes even meat. He didn't smoke, and we traded cigarette rationing tickets for food. We could trade like that until 1953 when rationing stopped. Of course, with the end of rationing came the devaluation of money, so we still couldn't buy much.

Being that Josef knew a lot of people, he sometimes got unexpected lifts. One day, the driver of a big truck stopped when he saw Josef bicycling along the road. The man invited him to hitch a ride. He put down the back gate and Josef rode his bike up on the back of the truck. The other riders were painters who had just finished a job painting a school. They had helped themselves to the leftover paint, which Josef saw shoved into the corner on the floor of the truck. Josef thought, "I can use some of this paint," and bought a can from one of them. When they stopped to let Josef out at Letka, they handed him down the paint can. Unfortunately, the lid was loose and the paint poured all over Josef. I was in the kitchen when I heard his yelling through the open window, "M-o-t-h-e-r!" That's the way he used to call me. I looked out of the window and there was a view fit for the gods—his hands and legs outstretched, his whole body covered with paint from top to bottom. Luckily, he wore a hat. I laughed, but what a job we had cleaning up that mess. His suit, we had to throw away. We wiped down the bike with almost an entire bottle of paint thinner, just to bring it back to a usable condition.

By far, Josef's greatest love was the accordion. When we were living in Liberec, Josef and his friends, Šnýdr and Berka (you may remember me mentioning Berka earlier), were able to put together a successful musical group. In the beginning, they had lots of opportunities to play. Innkeepers were always inviting them. Fortunately, the people there had simple tastes. I used to go with the three men to their performances, and afterwards we stayed overnight at a hotel. For several months, they went to Smržovka every Sunday afternoon, and sometimes I would accompany them. Berka was married, but I never met his wife. She couldn't join us because they lived way out in Dalimĕřice.

Šnýdr and Josef didn't know how to read notes; only Berka did. Their audiences liked them anyway. One assembly member from the Praha Parliament would always applaud and shake hands with each one of the musicians. Later, when there were plenty of good musicians around, hardly anyone was interested in hiring amateurs. With little demand, Josef and Šnýdr played whenever possible and for any amount of money they could get. Once in a while, somebody came to ask Josef to play for a wedding. When there was a wake in Turnov, Josef would take his accordion and I wouldn't see him for the next three days or until he recovered from his drunken binge.

But, for awhile, the three managed pretty well as long as Josef stayed sober. When he and his friends got drunk, it was terrible. Once, after they played in Česká Chalupa, they staggered home through the forest at night, got lost, and couldn't find their way out until morning. They really struggled lugging those musical instruments, especially Berka, who had to drag his heavy drums. Only Šnýdr had it easy; he only had to carry a violin.

How Josef met Šnýdr, I don't know. Šnýdr lived three railroad stations beyond Děčín. We went there once to take a look at where he lived. He had a nice, spacious little house, a small farm, a cow, and three children.

Šnýdr cheated Josef out of money at every opportunity. When they performed together, Šnýdr collected the tips, but never gave Josef his fair share of their earnings. It was easy to cheat Josef because he was always drunk by the end of the evening, and Šnýdr didn't drink. Once Josef returned home pale, poisoned by alcohol, and without his accordion. He didn't remember where he'd left it. He spent the entire next day in bed. He didn't eat and felt miserable. Only toward evening did he remember that he left his accordion in the locker room at the railroad station.

Josef's problem was that he was stupid, and that stupidity got him into a lot of trouble. For instance, there was the time when he traded a bicycle for a piece of an illegally killed pig. [Farmers were allowed to keep a certain number of animals, but regulations required them to register their animals with the state. Anything they did with the animals after that also had to be reported. If a farmer butchered a pig, that had to be reported and a small payment made to the state. It seems that no one had reported the change of status of this particular pig.] Somebody informed on Josef, and he had to pay a 1,500 crown fine.

Josef was cheated again when he agreed to lend 600 crowns to the manager of Collectable Materials. The manager recorded the reverse, that he lent 600 crowns to Josef. The man died suddenly and Josef had to pay 600 crowns to the manager's family, which they quite reasonably claimed he owed them. So he lost a total of 1200 crowns. On another occasion, he lent thirty skins to a collector and then never saw him or the skins ever again.

We finally ended up selling the house for 8,000 crowns, and we split the profits. It sounds like only a little, but after the devaluation, our 8,000 crowns actually was worth 40,000 crowns. We took some of the money and bought a new TV set for a nice apartment we moved into on Klášterní Street.

When I left Josef in 1953, he moved in with Marie, a former schoolmate of mine. That didn't hurt my feelings. By then, Josef was more like a son to me than a boyfriend. I cared more about him than for him.

For several months, they used to go to Smržovka every Sunday afternoon, and sometimes I would accompany them. Marie and Josef shared a small flat together that she owned in Turnov. After awhile, Josef took a job on the Jizera river, and Marie moved with him. His responsibility as a dam guard was to clean out the canals that got clogged with leaves in summer and with ice in winter. The position came complete with living quarters. When I went to visit them, I got off the train at Bozkov Station and walked through a pine forest along the Jizera river. It was quite far away, taking about an hour and a half to reach their house. The woods all around the dam kept everything dark and dreary, kind of sad looking. I didn't like how it felt, and it struck me that Josef wasn't going to be able to tolerate this place for long. He was used to mixing with many people, and now he would have to stay in this dreary, lonely place all day long.

The little building that served as their apartment sat in the middle of the dam. Josef and Marie had to bring in all their furniture and possessions by boat. Comforters, clothing, and everything else always felt damp. Heating their apartment was a big problem. For fuel, they had to cut down a tree, chop it into small pieces, and then split those pieces again.

Marie walked to work every day. Josef went to meet her in the evening halfway along the path because she was afraid to walk home alone in the forest after dark. As I thought, they didn't stay long at that place—perhaps a year.

When Marie died, Josef moved in with my sister, Růža, in Jičín. The two of them spent the last years of their lives in comfort, traveling and enjoying the good life. Josef died of a heart attack while he was pushing his bicycle through the gate of their home. Růža loved Josef very much. After his death in 1984, she lost weight rapidly and died four months later.

Josef's family, the Mužáks

Josef had five brothers and sisters. They were all crazy in one way or another. One of his sisters, Tereza, married an older man, and they lived near Boleslav. She made the mistake of trying to jump onto a moving train. Missing the step, she fell and her leg got caught under the train wheels. She lost the leg and became an invalid. After that, she spent most of her time on the couch. "A young, handsome priest often comes to visit her and brings her books to read," Josef's cousin, Gusta, would tell us with a wicked giggle.

The neighbors thought Josef's family was strange because every member of his family was a devout Catholic, unlike the majority of people around who were Catholic in name only. One evening in Turnov, in the days before I knew Josef, I saw the Mužák's family walking toward the church next to the cemetery. All of them were there, the three grandmothers and their families. I don't know what gave me the idea, but I followed them into the church. It was empty except for us. On one side were twelve pictures showing Jesus's life, including his crucifixion. As soon as the family entered the church, they knelt down in front of the first picture, and I did, too. They prayed and then shuffled on their knees to the next picture. I could only take it up to about the fifth picture, then I stood up and walked over to sit on a pew.

Chapter 11
On My Own Again

Jára's background notes
1929-1986

Mother's final letter containing memoirs was written when she was ninety-one, but that was only to answer my request to clarify some information from an earlier letter. Before that, her last detailed letter was written when she was eighty-eight. Sadly, Mother passed away in the summer of 2001 at the age of ninety-six, a month before, Sylvia Welner and I were scheduled to visit her in the Czech Republic. We went there anyway, and in her memory, walked through many of the small towns that played a prominent part in her life.

Mother's letter below discusses my brother, Mirek. He was a quiet, shy child. He tried to please my mother and not make her angry. (He was more worried about that than I ever was.) But even he was bound to not always listen to his mother, and he got into trouble, as Mother's letter describes.

The letter also mentions that when Mirek was old enough to get a job at the post office, my mother agreed to assist him by retrieving an official copy of her mother's birth certificate from the vicar of our local Catholic church. During that era, the Church served as the primary custodian of official documents, such as birth, marriage and death certificates.

Mirek needed to obtain a copy of his grandmother's birth certificate, rather than his own, as a requirement for government employment. The purpose for showing a grandmother's birth certificate was to rule out Jewish lineage. No Jews were allowed to hold government jobs under the Reich Protectorate of Bohemia and Moravia.

During and after the war, my mother and her community faced shortages of certain domestic goods and services. For instance, in the 1950s, stores in Czechoslovakia did not have washing machines for sale. But that didn't stop many Czech women, like my mother, from wanting them. Husbands and sons responded to these desires by rigging up machines from spare parts. Unfortunately, most men who built these washing machines didn't know much about electricity, so accidents, like the one described in my mother's letter, were common occurrences.

The brigades described by my mother were another phenomenon of that time. We participated in these work parties under the Nazis, but the Communist version demanded more of us in terms of time and loyalty. Under communism, we were frequently being mobilized into brigades to help collective farmers harvest their crops. We were told it was our patriotic duty. If there was a shortage of hands, the farmers could not go out and hire farm workers since employing others was illegal. Food was precious. We knew it was wrong to let it rot in the fields. So, like it or not, we fell victim to social pressure to be compliant volunteers.

Apartment space was also precious. Under communism, this space was allotted at a rate of twelve square meters (130 square feet) per person. As Mother discusses, if a tenant had a roommate who moved out, then he or she was out of luck. The only options were to find a replacement roommate or move.

For these reasons and others, the Communist era was a depressing time for most Czechs. Those with additional problems, such as serious chronic health problems, sometimes found it impossible to cope. We saw suicides escalating, exceeding even our historically high rate. They were only statistics—unless, of course, the victim happened to be a member of your own family.

My brother, Mirek, committed suicide. In the letters he left, he gave tuberculosis as the reason for his despondency. Maybe that was it, but I have a nagging feeling there was something more. I wonder whether, if I had been there, I could have intervened and averted this tragedy. Probably not, but I don't know and never will. That's what hurts so much and causes the heaviness in my heart whenever I think of him.

My decision to emigrate was difficult for many reasons, but staying would have been impossible. The rest of this introduction tells the story of that decision. My wife, Blanka, and I were reminiscing one day recently as we sat quietly having coffee in our home in Mission Viejo, California. "Jára," she said, "Do you remember long ago when we were traveling together on a train near Magdeburg passing through East Germany?"

I nodded slowly. On that day over forty years ago, I looked out the window as our train was approaching an underpass below the freeway that connected West Germany to West Berlin, a thoroughfare closed to the Communist world. I stared upward, amazed to see lines of cars carrying people driving freely to wherever they wanted to go. That was my first tangible evidence of the possibility of freedom.

It was that exposure to freedom, experienced several years before we decided to leave, that subconsciously planted the seed of possibility that we might some day emigrate to the West. My hunch is that half the Czech population considered leaving during those days, but only a small number actually did. People stayed for their own personal reasons. Of course, the few who maintained their faith in communism would want to remain. But, the majority had other reasons. For some, old age or health problems were deterrents. For others, family or school commitments were too strong to break. Patriotism or nationalism kept some in Czechoslovakia. Others were comfortable with their jobs and life style. Fear of the unknown, certainly including doubts about finding employment, and the dangers inherent in escape were also major obstacles.

Leaving our country meant leaving behind a lot of ourselves. Suddenly, we were separated from our home, family, friends, country, culture, language, and familiar places harboring happy memories. We knew it would be dangerous to try to escape. But the risk would be moderate compared to the peril faced by those people who made the attempt earlier, back when the Iron Curtain was pulled down tight.

During spring vacation in 1969, we drove to the mountains of Eastern Bohemia. We stayed there for a few days in a cottage in a mountainous area near the Polish border. One day, while we were exploring the region, we stopped at Suchý Vrch, a low, flat hill mostly covered with pastures. We strolled quietly in the pastureland while our daughters played on the grass. While we were walking, Blanka told me about a vivid dream she had had the night before: "I was in a city. Russian soldiers were everywhere. First, I was hiding in doorways, then I started running frantically. When I woke up, I realized this is the reality of what will be if we remain here. We will be running and hiding the rest of our lives. Not only physically, but hiding who we are inside." Blanka looked at me and said quietly, "I think we should leave Czechoslovakia." Those were words to my liking; I had been wanting to leave for a long time.

Although we both had professional jobs, almost all of our earnings went for food, clothing, and shelter. Our apartment was terrible, and there were no others available. These material deprivations were unpleasant, but they were not why we decided to leave our homeland.

What became truly unbearable, even more than having the Communists invade our public and personal life, was their intrusion into the privacy of our thoughts and beliefs. If they knew we didn't think favorably of them, we were immediately the enemy. They said, in essence, "You are either for us or against us." There wasn't any middle way. We all had to pretend that we were happy with communism. We had to vote for it. We could not speak against it.

The Communists developed a huge propaganda machine that permeated our lives: newspapers, radio, and later television; everything was propaganda. We were under constant pressure, brainwashed by an endless stream of talk about how nice life was under socialism and what the Communists were doing for the nation. This propaganda repeatedly compared the socialistic regime with capitalism, blaming America for all the ills of the world. We knew these were lies (although Blanka had been vulnerable to some of the propaganda). In fact, I came to believe that everything coming from the government must be a lie. But we couldn't say so in public. We had to pretend.

We were faced with the continual threat of losing our jobs if the Communists found out we were against them. Deception was the price of job security. Any dissent could cost us our jobs and land us in some place really terrible, like a coal mine. Passive compliance—not making waves—was not enough. We had to be loud and clear with our support of Communist ideology.

Teachers were especially affected. I know that from personal experience since I was teaching classes in silver smithing at the time. For teachers like Blanka and myself or others in influential roles, the government expected active participation in spreading the gospel of socialism [the foundation for communism under Marxist-Leninist theory]; what we privately thought or believed didn't matter. I was forced to incorporate comments about socialism into all of my classes. Regardless of the subject matter, I had to insert remarks about the glories of socialism and the horrors of capitalism. For instance, if I were lecturing on the technology of silver-working, I had to say something about how Capitalists use silver to manipulate society. I had to come up with some stupid lie. I didn't do it routinely; I tried to avoid it. But if an inspector came into the classroom, then I had to make my little speech. Although the hegemony gradually became less oppressive, the requirement to spread propaganda continued, especially in schools, during the whole period of that regime.

Blanka and I were sick of living a life of pretense. Our compelling reason for leaving was the intolerability of having to hide our true selves, pretending to believe in something we hated, perpetually living a lie. We were brought up to tell the truth; now we were liars. We feared for our sanity and personal integrity.[51] So we decided to leave at the end of the school year. This would give Blanka time to complete her degree in Special Education and give our daughters, Milena and Alena, time to finish their school year. Also, it would afford me the opportunity to complete my annual teaching responsibilities. In the interim, we agonized over the thought of separating from Mother and other family members—not knowing if we would ever see them again.

We took three months to plan our escape. All preparations had to be done secretly so that we wouldn't raise any suspicion. Blanka and I told our employers that we would like to visit Vienna for one week during summer vacation. They asked questions like, "What do you want to do there?" But eventually both sets of employers signed the necessary paperwork giving their permission for us to leave. We already had passports issued during Dubček's era under the act of free travel. But a passport was worthless by itself. The key was to obtain a travel permit from the governmental travel office. For the application to be accepted, two conditions had to be met. First, an employer had to sign the appropriate form (we were okay there) and second, an applicant needed an invitation from a relative or friend abroad who would agree to support the traveler during their stay if it became necessary. This latter condition made it difficult for many people, including us. (The rule was put in place because our government was afraid that Czechs traveling abroad might embarrass the Czechoslovak Socialist Republic by running out of funds.)

The invitation requirement was a problem for us, since we didn't know anybody in Austria. So we simply wrote the invitation ourselves and invented an imaginary friend to send it to us. Fortunately, I knew a Czech man who went to Vienna quite often to visit his aunt. I asked him to bring the letter of invitation with him the next time he went and mail it to me from there. He was too afraid to do this, but he was willing to bring me an envelope with an Austrian stamp and cancellation on it, and that was good enough. I put the fictitious letter that I wrote into the envelope, went down to the Government Travel Office, and told the clerk, "My wife and I need permits to leave Czechoslovakia. We want to travel to Austria."

Again, the same question, "What do you want to do there?"

I said, "We want to sightsee." I wasn't nervous; I was used to lying to the Communists. We got the permits.

The most realistic way to get to Vienna was by car, but our car was a Czech-built Praga Lady, over thirty years old and in terrible condition. The car was in such a poor state that we were afraid the Communists would bar us from taking it over the border—for fear that it would present an unfavorable image to the outside world. I turned to an ex-student of mine who tinkered around with cars whenever he had the opportunity. I trusted him and thought he could do a good job fixing up the Praga Lady. In exchange for his services, I promised to give him the car when we no longer needed it in Vienna. When we got the car back from him, we didn't recognize it; it looked almost like new. We were delighted.

Still, a few more problems had to be solved before we could go. We decided to leave all our possessions in our apartment. We couldn't give them to anybody because if our family or friends accepted our property, they would effectively become accomplices to our crime of escaping (called *leaving under false pretenses* by the authorities). We carefully transferred our money—which was worthless outside the country—into the hands of our relatives. Only a few people knew what we are doing: Blanka's parents, my brother and sister-in-law, and my friend who helped me fix up the car.

I had a long discussion with my brother, Mirek, and asked him to come with us. He said that he was not ready to leave the country he loved, where he was born. Not now anyway, maybe later, if and when things got worse. Although things did indeed get worse, he stayed until his death in 1986.

We wanted to take along our daughters. In fact, Blanka's ten-year-old daughter, Milena, did come with us. We took her without her biological father's knowledge or consent. Not surprisingly, when her father learned that we had taken his daughter, he was sad and upset. But over time he accepted our reasons and reluctantly agreed that it was probably for the best.

I managed to get the name of my daughter, Alena, on my passport, and we were ready to take her with us. During her last visit with Blanka and me in Praha before we left, we asked her if she would like to live with us rather than with her mother, with whom she was currently living. (We never mentioned leaving the country.) Alena couldn't make up her mind. Maybe we shouldn't have asked her; she was only eleven, but it was a huge decision for us to make without her consent. Due to her indecision and our presumption that her mother would be strongly opposed if she knew what we wanted to do, we decided not to take Alena with us. Leaving her behind was painful for me, knowing it might be years until I would see her again; however, at the time it seemed like the right thing to do.

What to do about my own mother was a distressing problem for me. In the end, I decided not to tell her our plans. Perhaps not surprisingly, she did sense something. In fact, she took the long train ride to Praha to talk me out of it. But I denied we were leaving. I am sorry that I lied to her, but I believed then and still believe today that we couldn't afford any additional risks. I intended to send for her later. (When I did twelve years later, she came to visit us in California, stayed for a few weeks, but couldn't wait to return to her homeland.)

My mother, I felt, could not have understood our urgency to leave the country. She had a different way of thinking about survival and the necessities of life. Growing up in a society where most people struggled just to feed, cloth, and shelter themselves, I didn't see how she could empathize with our need for self-fulfillment and authenticity. Politics and government were on the periphery of her life; she was only aware of them when they directly impinged on her daily routine. Experiencing a hardship-filled existence over a period of two world wars and two foreign occupations, she learned to co-exist with whatever was and to not internalize any more than was absolutely necessary. Blanka and I were able to change our level of aspiration only because we became the beneficiaries of improved security, physical comfort, and education. Blanka's parents were from my mother's generation, but they had the benefits of a higher level of education and material comforts, enabling them to relate to, we believed, the abstract reason that inspired us to seek a better life elsewhere.

The end of the school year was fast approaching. Blanka took her finals at the university while I graded my students' oral exams. We celebrated the end of the school year by having a party at one of Praha's nice restaurants. After the toast, the friend who fixed my car asked me jokingly if he should write to me in California. (Ultimately, we did end up in California, but neither he nor I could have sensibly guessed that at the time.) Fearfully, I looked around to see if anybody was listening. I whispered in his ear: *Drž hubu, ty vole!* (Shut up!).

Saying goodby to the home you love is a very personal experience. Blanka, thinking back to that time, has written the following description of her feelings shortly before our departure:

> I took a walk in Kampa, a beautiful part of Praha near the River Vltava. I enjoyed walking in this historic part of Praha, so quiet and peaceful, yet situated in the center of the city. The sky was grayish, like our life in those days. All happiness and joy—the sunshine and hope for a better future—were taken away from us the year before by the Russian military "helpers" who suppressed our reforms. I walked along talking to myself, deep in thought, looking into my heart.

Am I ready to take a leap into darkness not knowing how and where I'll land? Am I willing to take that risk? Yes, it can't be worse than this. I can't be happy in this country. I want to get out. I must always remember this moment, how I truly feel. I must never regret my decision. I must never idealize my life in this country when the hard times strike.

It was true. Hard times did come. But I have never forgotten the talk I had with myself that day while walking beside the river. Through the tough years, it has helped me overcome my doubts when I felt weak or self-pitying.

June thirtieth was the day of our departure. Blanka and I felt a sense of relief as we walked through our sixth floor attic apartment for the last time. Through our only window, we could see down to the cluttered backyard far below. Blanka, Milena and I descended the 160 steps (there was no elevator) to the street level where our car was waiting.

We stopped in Nusle to say goodby to Blanka's parents, not knowing that we were seeing her father for the last time. It was a very emotional moment for her, and she remembers it clearly:

My father was sixty-five then, younger than I am now. He was a tall man, his wavy hair pure white, rich and beautiful. We were holding hands and talking about the future. His hand holding mine was shaking. He was about to lose his only daughter and his granddaughter, too. Together, we were the joy of his life.

I loved my father. He was my confidant and trusted friend all of my life. My heart was breaking knowing how he was suffering over the idea of our leaving. I felt so much love and tenderness for him, yet there was nothing I could say to make the pain go away.

"When we settle down, you and mom will come to America to see us and stay with us as long as you wish." I needed to believe that it would happen one day. I did not want to see that he was frail and that he had not been feeling well for some time.

He kissed me and said softly, "Good-by, Blaninka. You've been a good daughter to me."

After saying our final farewells to Blanka's parents, we said goodby to the city of Praha we loved so much. We drove through the lovely Czech countryside toward the Austrian border and, by late afternoon, we reached Znojmo. That's when our car broke down. It refused to go any further, and we knew how difficult it would be to get it repaired quickly. Fortunately I found a mechanic who was willing to fix the car overnight for a hefty price. (I had plenty of crowns, soon to be useless, so I could afford it.) We checked into a hotel and waited.

The car was fixed in the morning as promised, and we continued on our way to the border. The watchtower and barbed wire appeared on our right, followed soon by the checkpoint. After inspecting our documents and asking a few questions, the officer in charge had me open the trunk. Next, he looked inside the car and even peeked under the car. He seemed satisfied. We had loaded the car with things a small family might use during a short summer vacation. We had no warm clothing with us because that would have looked suspicious since it was summertime. The officer walked three times around the car inspecting everywhere he could. Finding nothing unusual, he nodded for us to go. I stepped on the gas pedal and exhaled with relief. A few seconds later we were in the free world.

On the Austrian side, we didn't have any problem at the border passport checkpoint. The Austrian officer was courteous and brief, particularly in contrast to the Czech guard. He glanced at our car and said, "Okay," and waved us through. In a moment, we found ourselves charmed by the Austrian countryside with its tidy, clean villages. We continued driving slowly along until we came to a village where we made a brief stop to see an open-air market on the central square. There was some celebration going on that we didn't understand. Musicians attracted small clusters of passers by, while shoppers wandered in and out of the small shops selling all sorts of stuff. Before we left Praha, we were only allowed to exchange five dollar's worth of crowns for hard currency (U.S. dollars) at the bank. That was all the dollars we had, so we couldn't afford to buy anything. But we were nonetheless amazed at the abundance of everything.

Getting back into the car, we continued our drive to Vienna. Unfortunately, we had no idea where Vienna actually was. We had no map. I was navigating by instinct. The road led into a city, and I found a place to park and went into a shop to buy a map. The map, it turned out, was unnecessary; I had driven into the middle of downtown Vienna and was parked in front of the President's Mansion (the former palace of the Austro-Hungarian emperors).

We found that campgrounds were the cheapest lodging available: two dollars per night. That was good news since, remember, we had only five dollars and some practically worthless crowns. During our stay, I earned some money by helping the owner to erect a fence around his grounds. We lived there for three days.

We soon discovered an office run by the American Fund for Czechoslovakian Refugees, and they were a great help. They placed us rent-free on the fourth floor of an apartment house in central Vienna where we lived with other refugees. When we walked in, it looked to us like a typical apartment. There was a hall, to the left was a bathroom, to the right was a kitchen; there was a bedroom and then another bedroom. These would have been luxurious accommodations for our family if the apartment was just for us, but it housed thirty refugees. We didn't know anybody, and no one knew us.

The day after we moved into that apartment, I went to the Canadian Embassy and asked for asylum. Our plan had long been to emigrate to Canada. We had our hearts set on Vancouver. During the Prague Spring, we had an opportunity to see a travelogue on Canada made by a Czech producer. The Canada portrayed in that movie was a country of extraordinary natural beauty and mineral wealth. The film showed deposits of gold ore being discovered almost everywhere in Canada. There were scenes of buildings with twenty-four karat gold faucets as evidence of Canada's geological fortune. The movie also portrayed Canadians as enjoying a high standard of living illustrated by a scene showing shoppers buying whole chickens for a dollar apiece. The fact that chicken was so reasonably priced calmed Blanka's fears, reassuring her that her family wouldn't starve in Canada.

Of course, we were vulnerable to misinformation from years of having no access to information from the free world. Only those who were members of the Communist Party were allowed to travel abroad, so we had no way of separating truth from fiction. The rest of us could only guess.

So it was with some disappointment that we received the news from the Canadian Embassy official: "It is difficult for you to get a Canadian visa now. Last year, Canada was open for all immigrants from Czechoslovakia; but this year, it's limited. Canada requires you to have $400 per person to qualify," he told us. Of course, we didn't have that kind of money. The Canadians recommended that we emigrate to the United States, which was then quite open to refugees from Eastern Europe. My immediate reaction was that the U.S. was even better than Canada, but Blanka was less pleased. Blanka had read several books by American authors that talked about the problem of homeless people in America. These books described people with no money living under bridges with no shelter or anything to eat. She imagined that we would suffer the same fate since we didn't have any money either.

Furthermore, in Vienna at that time, many people were anti-American. They also had read books about the homeless in America and heard other opinions that made them disdainful of Americans. Austrian acquaintances told Blanka that Americans have no manners or graces. To illustrate the point, they said that Americans don't hold their knife in their right hand and their fork in their left the way Europeans do when they eat. Instead, Americans eat with their forks and pick up their knives only when they need to cut a piece of meat. Austrians joked about the Americans' lack of proper manners as stemming from their cowboy past. They laughed about cowboys in western films having a fork stuck in the top of their boots. The message was that that's the way Americans were—gross, with no European refinements. "You wouldn't be happy there," they told Blanka.

I did not share Blanka's wariness. Besides, we really had no options, so we went down to the American Embassy. They gave us a written application and asked us various questions like, "Are you a member of the Communist Party?" We were clean in that respect. They verified everything anyway. Then they sent us to take a tuberculosis test. That was the American Embassy's only health concern. After that, all went smoothly, and we were put on a waiting list.

Our apartment was in the center of Vienna, so everything was accessible. The refugee agency also managed to get jobs for us. Blanka started to work as a cleaning lady in the Central Bank, the major bank of Austria. It was her job to scrub all the floors in the building and also to clean the men's and women's restrooms.

Under the Communists, we were taught that all labor was noble. Blanka thought she believed that but, until then, never was put to the test. Notwithstanding the philosophy of the Communist system in Czechoslovakia, Blanka and I were well educated professionals and therefore considered somebodies. Now Blanka was a nobody. Standing unobtrusively in the corner of the restroom holding a rag mop and bucket of soapy water, she couldn't help feeling indignant. It pained her to watch those young tellers in their business suits standing in front of the restroom mirror freshening up their makeup and putting on lipstick just like she used to do. Now, she was the invisible cleaning lady. Thinking back, Blanka recalls, "The sudden change from being a respected professional to scrubbing public toilets forced me to learn a lot about myself. I realized that I had been a snob, but I didn't know it. That experience 'unsnobbed' me."

Blanka's feelings, the violations to her self-esteem, were not just about having to clean other people's toilets and wash feces smudges off the walls of the men's stalls. There was more to contend with than that. She was an attractive thirty-seven-year-old woman, and the male employees at this prestigious bank felt at liberty to take advantage of her. Finding her in the office area with her mop and pail, they would regularly trap her behind one of the many file cabinets and make indecent advances toward her. Although she managed to wiggle out of these situations, they were stressful and humiliating. In Austria during those times, neither her employer nor the laws of the nation offered her any protection. Blanka's only safety lay in her own cleverness to find a way out without losing her job, which she couldn't afford to do.

To distract herself from her troubles and at the same time do something useful, she decided to work on her English vocabulary. (Blanka and I were fairly fluent in German, although we did not like to speak it. We associated it with the Nazi occupation and the compulsory German language classes we were forced to take in school.) She brought a Czech-English dictionary to work and while she was mopping, she recited the new words she was learning out loud, pairing them in Czech and English couplets. With a page torn from the dictionary taped to the top of her mop stick, she started with the letter A and worked her way forward through the alphabet. By the time she left the bank, Blanka had learned all the words through the letter H. That was her vocabulary in English, words A-H. Admittedly, this was incomplete, but compared to me she was an accomplished linguist.

Her job at the bank was close enough to our apartment for her to walk to work. I got a job, too, as a helper in a shop where they made custom electrical panels. The pay was not very good, but together we made enough to live on, since we paid no rent. We survived on the cheapest food available: bread, lentils, and liver.

Vienna was a beautiful city. I'd get up early in the morning and walk about forty minutes to my place of work. I couldn't afford public transportation, so I always walked. Each morning, I'd choose a different route and see another part of Vienna. I really enjoyed that.

Milena, being ten years old at the time, was able to be on her own during the day. She stayed in the apartment and played with the other kids there. Occasionally, she accompanied her mother to work, following behind Blanka as she scrubbed the floors in the large cavernous bank building.

We lived like this for only four months, the summer months; it was beautiful, sunny and warm in Vienna. We were looking forward to our future life in the United States, so the wait passed quickly. It was a hard time, but it was a good time. In any case, we were lucky. Some people waited a year, or even longer, for a visa.

While in Vienna, I found the name and address of a former Czech refugee, Jerry Barnet, on a list of refugees provided to us by the agency that had placed us in our apartment. These refugees, now relocated in America, were willing to assist new émigreés. Although Mr. Barnet was a complete stranger to us, we wrote to him in Sherman Oaks, California. He answered, and we exchanged several letters. He was very kind and helpful; he even promised to assist us when we arrived in California. Finally, we sent him a letter saying that we were coming on a certain day. We received no reply. For some unknown reason, we lost contact with Mr. Barnet at a most critical time, just when we found out our departure date.

On October 27, 1969, we boarded an old, leaky charter plane that soon filled up with refugees. I remember that as we flew through the clouds water dripped on us from the ceiling. Most of the Czechs on the plane expected to end up in New York, New Jersey, or Chicago. We hoped for California. Blanka and I didn't know where we would spend our first night in America, let alone our final destination. (We certainly didn't expect it to be Los Angeles.) We made a short stopover in Brussels, and then started our flight over the Atlantic to New York.

This was the first airplane trip for all three of us. My whole body was tense, and my eyes were darting everywhere. But soon I realized that we were already free, traveling like those people on the West German freeway we stared at enviously from our East German train window years ago. After that, I enjoyed the flight in spite of the uncertainties about what lay ahead. Milena also enjoyed the flight; she was fascinated with the dispensers in the tiny bathrooms on the plane where she could playfully squirt soap, powder, cologne, or hand lotion on her hands.

I remember our first steps on American soil. Our plane was directed to some remote corner of Kennedy Airport. Soon we were walking briskly along the asphalt pavement past some ugly, inhospitable buildings. Customs procedures were short. Before we knew it, we found ourselves in a big hall full of people. Unexpectedly, we heard our name on the public address system. A man approached us and, speaking to us in Czech, told us that our plane to Los Angeles would be leaving at eight o'clock in the evening and to wait right where we were for somebody to take us and our luggage to the proper terminal. Our friend, Jerry Barnet, hadn't forgotten us after all.

We did as instructed, but the departure time was approaching and nobody showed up to take us to our terminal. Then it was eight o'clock, eight-ten, eight-twenty and still nobody came. Finally a heavyset, black man appeared and said in English, "Here are three tickets to Los Angeles." He took our luggage, tossed it into the trunk of a huge taxi cab, seated us inside, and drove off to our terminal. Although we did not understand well, he used enough A-H words and pantomime for Blanka to figure out what he was trying to tell us: the wall clock in the waiting room was not yet readjusted for the end of daylight savings time.

The flight to Los Angeles was a more comfortable one than the first leg of our journey. There was enough room on the plane for Blanka, Milena, and me to each choose a row and spread out comfortably. When I woke up, we were approaching the Los Angeles airport. A myriad of lights from the sprawling city greeted us.

We decided that, upon landing, we would take a bus to Sherman Oaks where Jerry Barnet lived. We didn't realize how difficult it would be in that huge city to get from one point to another by bus. Nor did we ever think that busses might not be operating at that late hour. It was close to midnight.

Fortunately, Barnett greeted us as soon as we stepped into the airport waiting room. He told us that he was going to take us to a temporary apartment on Western Avenue in Hollywood. On the way there, we stopped at a small restaurant on Wilshire and Western where Jerry ordered strawberry shortcake for all of us. It was the best cake we had ever eaten. We told him that we were amazed that he was able to find us so quickly at the airport. "How did you recognize us?" we asked.

He said, "Oh, you had that shabby old luggage. I thought, it must be you." With four hundred dollars in our pocket, and those two pieces of worn luggage, we started a new life in California.

In the years that followed, Mother and I kept in close contact through letters. From 1990 on, I visited my mother every few years, grateful for her relatively good health and ability to still carry on conversations with me. I last saw her in the spring of 1997. At that time, I told her that my friend was writing a book about her, based on her letters to me. "Why would someone want to write about me?" she asked incredulously.

Tonča's letter to Jára

Finally, I learned my lesson. From age forty-eight on, I lived like a nun. This was in spite of the many men who were interested in me, especially when I was living in Liberec working at the Varšava Cinema on Moskevská Street.

Working in the cloakroom

Studenecký, the projectionist at the Varšava Cinema, wasn't a romantic interest of mine, but I remember him because he was so peculiar. When Studenecký was a young man living in Turnov, he was engaged to a girl from Daliměřice. She lived with her mother in a small house on a street by the stairs leading down to the Jizera River. A few days before their wedding day, he was riding down the highway on his motorcycle with his bride-to-be seated in back with her arms wrapped around his waist. They were on their way to shop for a wedding veil. But they never reached the store. There was an accident—Studenecký crashed into a guard stone on the road beyond Turnov, not far from Sedmihorky—and the girl was killed. How that could have happened on a straight highway, I don't know. Maybe he was drunk, because later on he drank a lot. He used to be a skilled watchmaker, but he stopped working at that trade. His drinking could have been the cause of that, too.

The last time I saw him was the day he was drunk on the job at the Varšava Cinema. The audience noticed the picture moving in a strange way and then, total darkness. Several men ran into the projection booth and found him and his co-worker drunk, slumped over among rolls of film scattered across the floor. The manager fired both of them.

I worked as an attendant in the cloakroom of that cinema for twelve years. They had two shows every day except on Sundays when they had three. I liked my job, but it gave me a hernia. In the tight little cloakroom, I had to shuffle the heavy coats that came in and went out at the beginning and end of each performance. One evening, the other cloakroom attendant stupidly put three coats on one hook. When I went to lift the top two heavy overcoats off the hook to get to the bottom one, something in me tore.

The manager of the theater was a devoted Communist who organized compulsory work brigades on a regular basis. We were expected to harvest the flax growing in the many fields around us. The manager also had us pulling weeds and mowing the grass in the summer open-air amphitheater. She never paid us a single crown for that work. After she died, we rarely participated in brigades.

My next cloakroom job was at the Imperial Hotel. Besides checking coats, we made money selling cigarettes and souvenirs. The lady I worked with advised us, "Keep your eyes open for the tourist buses. Those folks buy a lot, but to make sales, you'll have to be quick." I didn't like the pressure, and so I quit.

A week later, I noticed a sign *Cloakroom attendant wanted* outside a small children's theater. I walked in, asked for the job, and they hired me on the spot. I worked there eight years.

Living with Alena

Although I enjoyed working at the theater, I eventually had to leave. Your daughter, Alena, needed me after her mother died in 1971. She was only fourteen then, too young to live alone. She and her mother had been living together in Moravia (a long train ride for me) since your divorce in 1964. With you remarried and living in California, it fell on me to stay with Alena. Her only means of support came from the money you sent her each month. She wanted to keep her apartment, but the rules did not allow that for a minor or a single person living in a two-person flat. I stayed with Alena in Moravská Třebová for several months until the family could figure out what to do. I left when her uncle, who was a big shot in the Communist Party, made arrangements for her guardianship.

Alena was never happy with anything I did. We had a stormy relationship, so I was relieved to leave and return to my apartment in Liberec. But with me gone, the government made her move from her apartment for two into a smaller one. She never forgave me for that.

Working for a commercial laundry

As soon as I returned home from Alena's, I began looking for a job. I found one in a large laundry facility in Růžodol. (Now I can see its high chimney from my window.) I lived on Klášterní Street then, and Růžodol was a long distance to travel to work. At the beginning, I liked working in the small laundry room preparing napkins and towels for the press. It was a good job and paid quite well (eight crowns per hour). I even had a half-hour break. There was a room with showers as well as a bathtub for employee use. Many of the young women hid there to smoke and avoid work.

Later, the manager put me in a larger laundry room. Instead of working by myself, I had to pair up with another woman to pull the heavy wet bedspreads tightly before they went to the press. That work was too hard for me. My hernia started to hurt again, so I had to leave that job.

The washing machines of the '50s

In the '50s, we didn't have plumbing. When we wanted to wash clothes, first we had to heat the water for the washing machine. The laundry room, next to my flat, had a stove for that purpose. One sunny day, I was getting ready to use the washing machine, so I filled the stove with the plastic cups I had collected for fuel and put some newspapers on top. I tossed in a match and went out to the line to collect an earlier wash load, now clean and dry. Suddenly, I heard a loud bang coming from the laundry room. I peeked in and saw that the blast had knocked a big hole in the wall between the laundry room and my apartment. Plastic cups were not the thing to burn, I learned. The explosion twisted the pipe to the chimney and left big pieces of concrete all over the floor. It certainly would have killed me if I had been still standing in the laundry room.

Later, Mirek and his friend built me an electric washing machine. After a while, the electric current started leaking and giving me little shocks. Once I was doing the laundry with leather shoes on when some inner voice told me to put on rubber overshoes. So I did. I barely touched the washing machine when I immediately flew through the air, ending up on my back on the floor. Always something protected me, maybe a miraculous gene.

Whatever power that usually protected me didn't do its work when it came to hernias. I developed my second hernia when I was sixty-five. One day, I was cleaning my little room and noticed that the linoleum under the bookshelf was wet. I wanted to remove the linoleum, but it wouldn't come loose. I pulled with all my might and felt something break inside me. It didn't hurt much, but later I noticed a bulge developing.

My stay in the hospital

It was in 1984 when I spent ten days at the hospital with a condition having nothing to do with hernias. My doctor sent me to Kosmonosy, but not because I was crazy. It was because of my nerves and depression. I guess he was worried. He knew of my history of attempted suicides, including the one recently when I tried to overdose on sleeping pills. As usual, I bungled the job.

I didn't have a single minute of decent sleep in Kosmonosy. I lay in the corner of a big room with folding beds to the right of me. At the foot of my bed was a w.c.. All night long, women were passing in and out of my room and other rooms on their way to and from the toilet. The younger women smoked and even fought in the w.c.. The two night nurses who worked the floor had their transistor radio blaring continually, and I suspect they even slept during their shift. It was an absolute horror!

When Mirek came and saw how I looked, he signed a release form and took me home. Later, I visited a local psychiatrist who gave me two little brown pills to take daily. Those pills didn't help my shattered nerves a bit. I got worse and worse, so the doctor ordered me back to the hospital. I waited the entire day at the main hospital for transportation to Kosmonosy. I finally arrived there in the evening, and a very pleasant doctor met me in the reception area.

The doctor asked me many questions, including arithmetic problems, to check my mental state. When I answered all of them correctly, she told me that I didn't belong there. She offered to send me home immediately if the ambulance was still around. Fortunately, it wasn't, and I remained at the hospital. My doctor said, "Since you have to stay, I'm giving you two powerful pills that will make you sleep well." She took me to a room where there were six older women. In the morning, she asked me, "Did you sleep well?"

I replied, "I would have if it weren't for the noisy women queued up to use the w.c.. They leaned against my bed and kept waking me up." So the doctor moved me to another room that was smaller, where only four women shared the w.c.. Finally I got a peaceful night's sleep. I stayed in this room for five days; then Mirek came for me. To this day, I take those same pills, although now they don't work as well.

Mirek as a child

Jára, when you were a young boy, I took you and your brother to a fair in Jeníšovice. We stopped to look in a stall where they were selling inexpensive jewelry, and you bought me a simple piece with two little hearts on it. One heart I lost. I am looking right now at the remaining heart. I still treasure it. It's not unlike my own heart, half torn out so long ago when I lost Mirek. But I can't think about that; the pain is too unbearable.

Mirek was only eleven months when he started to walk. On that day, he let go of the bar on the side of the baby carriage and took his first few steps. He toddled over toward the table where I used to do my jewelry-making work. I'm sorry for not appreciating those special moments more back when they were happening.

Before Mirek was of school age, I sent him to a nursery school, but only occasionally. I didn't like that the school was so far away. I preferred to leave him with Konůpek when I needed to run some errands. It never bothered him to babysit you children. He continued working, making his shoes, while you and Mirek watched in fascination. Before Mirek was born, it was you, Jára, who sat by Konůpek's side and watched him work.

One afternoon after Papa's death, I noticed that Mirek wasn't around. I looked outside the house and around the neighborhood, but couldn't find him anywhere. Since he was only four years old, I was quite upset. Suddenly, I thought of going to his nursery school to look for him. It was quite a distance, about a half hour walk. He was there, all right. He had wandered off on a familiar path and landed in front of his classroom.

I also remember sending Mirek to Šulc, the baker, to ask him to bake me some Christmas cakes. I made the dough myself and wanted him to form it and bake it into loaves for us. Mirek went back when they were ready to be picked up, and on the way home, he nibbled on the edges. As he handed me the cakes, I saw there were small chunks missing here and there. I am glad now that I didn't spank him or even scold him. I only remember that he looked at me pleadingly and whispered, "They smelled so good." It was wartime, and you and Mirek rarely had much in the way of treats.

Youngsters at that time used to catch rides by hanging on to the back of horse-drawn carriages. Traveling that way was convenient and cheap. Mirek especially liked to do this when he was coming to a hill. With one hand, he would hold on to his bike and, with the other, grab hold of the back of the carriage ahead of him. I'd tell him, "Mirek, that's dangerous," but he didn't listen.

When Mirek was eight years old, he was walking along and decided to hitch a ride by jumping onto the back of a carriage. When he reached his destination, he jumped off, not realizing how close he was to a passing motorcycle. The driver slowed, but couldn't avoid smacking into him. In 1937, a few years before World War II, motorcycles were just appearing on the streets. There weren't very many, but one of them struck Mirek and broke his shoulder bone.

Mirek earned good grades in school so I bought him a pair of skis as a reward. That made him very happy; he loved to ski. When I think back to Mirek's childhood, I feel sad. There are many things that I wish I had done differently, like appreciating and protecting him more when he was young. As I should have for you too, Jára. That is why life holds no pleasure for me.

My visit to the rectory for Mirek

It was in 1943, when Mirek was fourteen, that he got his first real job—a position at the post office. Before he could report to work, he needed my help because of a special requirement in those days for anyone wishing a government job. That's why the postal inspector asked Mirek to bring in his grandmother's official birth certificate. I didn't have it at home; my mother's birth certificate was stored at the rectory. To get it, I had to ride my bicycle past Jičín to Podhradí and then find my way to the rectory. When I got there, the vicar was just climbing into a buggy where two men were already seated. The vicar called down to me, "Come back later. I have to go now." And he drove off. I didn't have a chance to tell him how long I'd traveled to get there, what I wanted, or that I only needed a few minutes of his time. Instead, I had to wait there all alone until he returned that evening.

It was a sweltering day, so I walked into the church where it was cool and slipped into a back pew. At first, I felt uncomfortable sitting there. This was the church where my mother used to come every week to pray. I imagined *maminka* sitting in exactly the spot where I was seated.

I had on a light summer dress, and I started to feel chilled. I stood up and walked outside. Soon I realized how hungry I was. Not knowing how long I'd be stuck there, I hadn't thought to bring food or ration coupons to buy something to eat. It started to get dark. Finally, to my relief, the vicar returned, and he gave me the birth certificate. That night, instead of riding all the way home, I stayed with Růža in Jičín.

Scarlet fever

Soon after that trip to the rectory, I became violently ill. There were only a few doctors in our town during the war. Doctor Havlín, my Czech doctor, was on vacation, so I had to go to the doctor in the German army barracks who was covering for him. He gave me some pills, but they didn't help. I had a high fever and a terrible thirst which lasted for two weeks. By the time Dr. Havlín returned, I felt better, but I visited him anyway because I still couldn't stop drinking. He noticed that I had a rash on my hands and asked, "Do you have the same rash on your feet?"

"Yes," I answered.

"Well, you've had Scarlet Fever," said Dr. Havlín.

Little by little, the rash and my constant thirst disappeared and I completely recovered—no thanks to any doctor.

Mirek's engagement to a patient from the sanatorium

It was in 1955, I remember, when Mirek wanted to marry Anina. She was a patient at Wolker's Sanatorium in Liberec, high in the mountains. It was a place with clean air, good for recovering tuberculosis patients. (Now the air is no longer fresh. It is polluted from the smoke blowing over from the factories in Poland, across the border.) Anina met Mirek in town during one of her daily walks and little by little got to know him. One day, he brought her over to my flat to meet me. When she was leaving our house, Anina turned around at the door to face me and in a chilly voice announced, "I officially invite you to the wedding."

Anina was from a big farm in Kroměříž where she lived alone with her mother. Mirek knew nothing about farm life. The only thing he ever did that in any way resembled rural living was to buy a gun to shoot sparrows. The wedding never took place because of some feelings on Anina's side of the family. I suspect that her mother wanted Anina to marry someone with experience running a large farm.

Not long after Mirek and Anina canceled their engagement, Mirek decided to sell his gun. He only wanted it when he thought he was going to be living out in the country. A young man came to see the gun one day when I was home by myself. He picked it up and aimed it at me. "What if I shoot you?" he said. Well, he didn't. Neither did he buy it. He just put it down and left. Was the fellow crazy? I don't know, but he certainly scared me. I was really lucky because I found out later the gun was loaded.

Mirek lived with me for some time in Liberec until he was able to find a small flat of his own. I used to go there to clean up his place for him. He later exchanged that flat for a larger one in Praha-Žižkov.

Sadness in the world

Jiřina and Mirek dated for eight years before he married her on December 9, 1963. After their wedding, they lived in her tiny flat in Králův Háj [Liberec]. Mirek visited me very often. Officially, on the books, they lived with me because it gave me some rent advantages. I could keep my flat if it looked like the three of us were living there together. Apartments still were controlled by the government, and the same restrictions still applied. Later, Jiřina and Mirek moved to Praha where Mirek got a job at a major bank (Živnostenská Banka) doing whatever electrical work they needed. He said something about computers, but I don't know what that's all about.

When Mirek came to visit me last, I offered him 100 crowns to help him with his finances. He didn't take it. In the past, he accepted money to help pay for gasoline. This time, he looked at me sadly. He said, "I don't need any money." Now, I always see that look in my mind's eye and cry. Why is he gone while I am still living?

[A few hours after Mirek's visit to his mother, he was dead. His family found him in his garage in Praha several days later. He had closed the garage door with the motor running. In letters he left behind, he said the reason he took his life was because of the reappearance of tuberculosis, an illness he had been suffering from for many years on and off. Jára thinks there were other reasons, but no one will ever know. His mother never was told the true nature of Mirek's death.]

My mother died on November 14, 1919 and my father on November 9, 1937. All of my sisters are gone: Máňa died in July of 1936, Anča on May 25, 1967, Julča on November 9, 1982, and Růža on April 15, 1984. Mirek passed away in November, 1986. Four of our family members died in the month of November. Nobody knows how much sadness I've had in this world. It's my turn now, and I'm ready to go.

APPENDIX

Major Historical Events Time Line

1914	First World War starts.
1916	Emperor Franz Josef I dies and is succeeded by Karl I.
1918	End of First World War; Czechoslovakia achieves nationhood.
1933	Adolf Hitler comes to power in Germany.
1935	T. G. Masaryk resigns as first president of Czechoslovakia and Dr. E. Beneš elected president.
1938	Germany occupies Austria.
1938	Munich Treaty allows Germany to occupy Czech border territory (Sudetenland).
1939	Hitler invades western part of Czechoslovakia and makes that region the Protectorate of Bohemia and Moravia under his control.
1939	"Independent" State of Slovakia established (puppet state under Hitler's control).
1939	Hitler invades Poland; Second World War starts.
1942	Reichsprotektor Heydrich assassinated by Czech partisans. Tremendous German repression follows; village of Lidice leveled, men shot to death, women and children taken to concentration camp. Massive persecution of the Jews.
1945	End of Second World War in Czechoslovakia. Russian army enters our country and liberates us from the Germans.
1948	Political nonviolent takeover of Czech government. It went from democracy to Communism when Czech Communists seized power through an arranged putsch engineered by Soviets.

1968   In January, Communist party leader Alexander Dubček, enacted reforms: "Socialism with a Human Face." This liberation movement was called *Prague Spring*.

1968   In August, *Prague Spring* crushed by Soviet military intervention.

1989   End of Communist rule in Czechoslovakia.

1993   Peaceful division of Czechoslovakia into separate states of Czech Republic and Slovakia.

Tonča's Ancestors and Siblings

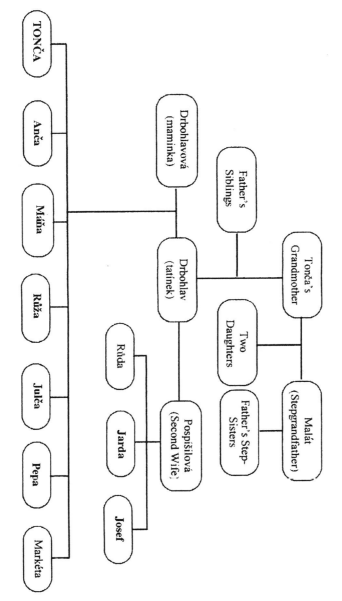

Tonča's Post-Marriage Family

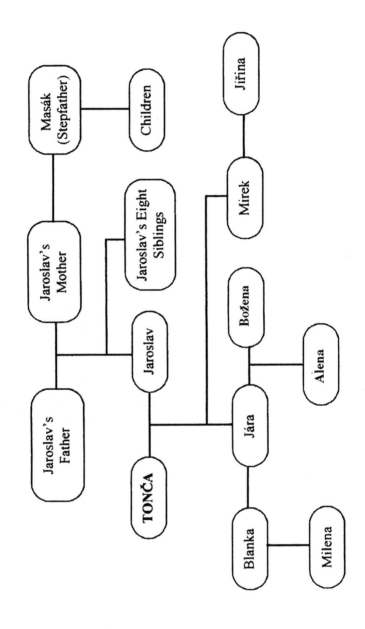

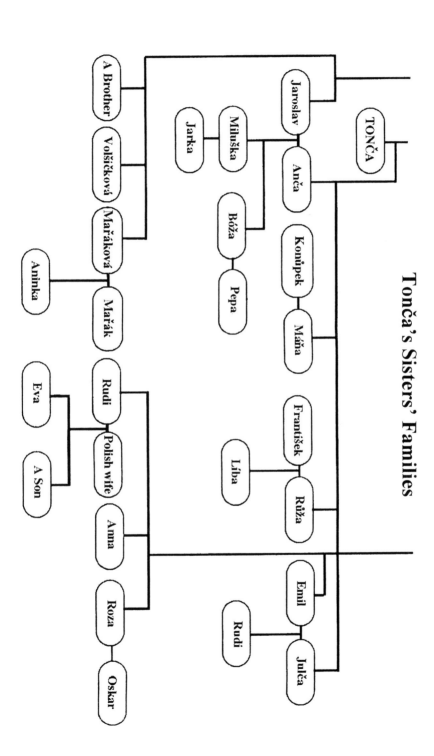

Tonča's Sisters' Families

Region Map

GERMANY   POLAND

CZECHOSLOVAKIA
(CZECH REPUBLIC)

Liberec
Jablonec

Daliměřice
Turnov
Rovensko
Ktová
Libuň
Jičin

Mladá Boleslav

Prague   Vienna
35KM   260KM

0   5   10   20   30KM

Sketch of Rovensko Area

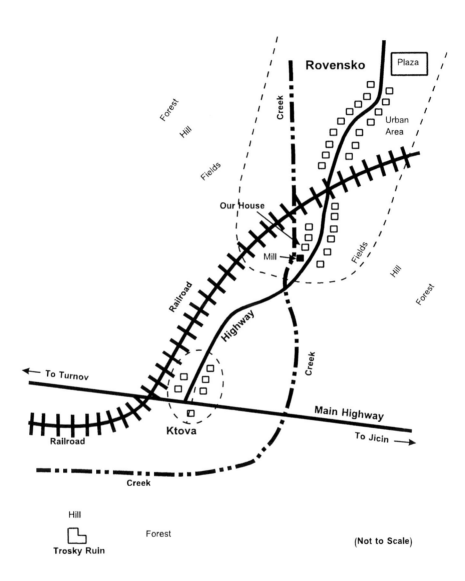

NOTES

1. Derek Sayer, *The Coasts of Bohemia* (Princeton: Princeton University Press,1998), 16.

2. Patricia Hampl, *A Romantic Education* (Boston & New York: Houghton Mifflin Company, 1981), 188.

3. The Rovensko pod Troskami web site is in Czech. From the home page, <http:// www.Rovensko.cz>, the current population figure is found in "základní informace" or by going directly to <http:// www.Rovensko.cz/rovensko_basic.htm>

4. *Seznam míst v království Českém.* Statistics for Rovensko pod Troskami in 1907 were: 2,143 inhabitants, 373 homes, all of Czech ethnicity. In 1913, they were: 2, 244 inhabitants, 399 homes, no change in ethnicity. See also, "1. Země Česká," *Statistický Lexikon Obcí v Republice Československé* (Praha, 1934): 377. The census report of 1930 shows a population decrease that brought the population figure down to 1,708.

5. Sayer, 66. Servile land tenure ended in 1848.

6. "A Wonderful Spring! Thompson's Bromine Arsenic Water Springs in Ashe County, NC," *New River Notes.* Excerpt from an advertisement published in 1887 by Eli Barker for what became known as Healing Springs, Coupler, Ashe County, North Carolina. <http://www.ls.net/~newriver/nc/heal1887.htm>, (9 July 2003).

7. Joanne Sala, ed. *Czech Proverbs* (Iowa City: Penciled Press, 1994) 62.

8. Sayer, 168.

9. Ibid.

10. Ibid., 165-6. See also Hampl, 185-6.

11. Hampl, 183-4.

12. Francis Conway and Patrick Box all, *Support for Small Municipalities in the Czech Republic.* (Washington, D.C.: The Urban Institute, SAID Project,1994), iii and 1-3. Report was prepared for International City County Management

Association, Local Government and Housing Privatization, <http://www.dec.org/pdf_docs/PNACC514.pdf>

13. Hampl, 216-217. Hampl gives an easy to read description of Hus and his church.

14. Sayer, 46.

15. Catholic Encyclopedia, *Leitmeritz, II Statistics.* In 1909, Northern Bohemia had 309 German parishes, as compared to 95 Czech parishes. (There were some mixed parishes, too.) <http://www.newadvent.org/cathen/09141a.htm>

16. The Evangelical Church of Czech Brethren, *History* (Praha, Czech Republic: Ecumenical Council of Churches in the Czech Republic, 2001), <http://www.ekumenickarada.cz/erceng/cce.html>

17. The Embassy of the Czech Republic, *Religion,* <http://www.mzv.cz/Washington/general/general.htm> See also Jim and Laurie Barnes, "The Czech Spiritual Landscape in the Post-Communist Era," *East-West Church & Ministry Report,* Spring 1996, 6-8, <http://www.samford.edu/groups/global/ewcmreport/articles/ew06205.htm> (20 June 2004).

18. Alan L. Berman, "Suicide," *Microsoft Encarta Online Encyclopedia* (2004), <http://encarta.msn.com/encyclopedia_761555737/Suicide.html>

19. Václav Havel, *Disturbing the Peace* (New York: Alfred A. Knopf, 1990), 188.

20. Radio Prague Internet, *Jablonec nad Nisou,* <http://archiv.radio.cz/mapa/more.phtml?mesto=8> (20 June 2004).

21. Město Jablonec nad Nisou, *Town History* (author unknown). Městský úřad Jabonec nad Nisou, Czech Republic, <http://www.mestojablonec.cz/mesto/historie_en.php> (20 June 2004).

22. Sayer, 50.

23. Ibid, 106-7.

24. Ibid, 66-67.

25. *Colliers Encyclopedia*, v.9, 62, "Germany: Bismark and Unification," P.F. Colliers & Son Corporation, w.o.s. (New York, 1959).

26. Sayers, 113-116.

27. *Statistický Lexikon obcí v Republice Československé,* Vydán ministerstvem vnitra a Státním úřadem statistickým, "1. Země Česká," (Praha, 1934): 113. 1930 census showed Jablonec nad Nisou with a population of 33,958. The ethnic break down was 16.5% Czech, 79.56% German, and a total of 3.94% others.

28. Hampl, 259-260. Quoting Růžena Hampl's memoir: "Without music, without books and movies, what am I?" she said. "I'm nothing. Without culture, nothing. I must have that. Food, no. Culture, I have to have." See also *World literacy rates: 2002-2003,* Asa Hilliard, <http://www.ideal-group.org/Literacy_Rates.htm> (26 June 2004).

29. "Total Mobilization, Resistance, and the Holocaust," *German Culture*. This excerpt explains how Germany was reorganized for total mobilization to support the war effort, <http://www.germanculture.com.ua/library/history/bl_holocaust.htm> (23 June 2004).

30. Radio Prague - the International Service of Czech Radio. *Radio Prague - 65 years*. <http://www.radio.cz/en/html/65_clouds.html> (23 June 2004).

31. Tony Valach, "Vera Masa Biographical Sketch," *Tucson Czech-Slovak Club Newsletter* (2004).

"Vera recalls listening to Radio Free Europe on shortwave; however, the Nazis declared that behavior *verboten* and required all radios brought in and the shortwave capability neutralized. '. . but leave it to the resourceful Czechs,' Vera says, '. . . they found out if you somehow put in a coin, it would connect; but we always had to have someone watch, for if we got caught, it was jail and even death.'" <http://tucsonczechslovak.homestead.com/Newsletter2.html>

32. Sayers, 231.

33. Ibid., 231-232.

34. NJMS National Tuberculosis Center, "Brief History of Tuberculosis" (New Jersey: 1996). The name *consumption* comes from the word *phthigis*. In 460 BC, Hippocrates said that it was the most widespread disease of the time and almost always fatal. <http//www.umdnj.edu/~ntbcweb/history.htm> (28 June 2004).

35. Ceeroosh Hartunian, M.D., interview by author, Manhattan Beach, CA. An x-ray can reveal scars from a subclinical case of tuberculosis. (6 April 2000).

36. "Semolina info Cooking Tips," *Lovely Recipes*. Mashed semolina is still used in many countries as a weaning food, <http://www.lovelyrecipes.com/cooking-tip.php?recipeid=2687>

37. "Spas," *Czech Republic: Ministry of Foreign Affairs*, 2002, <http://www.czech.cz/index.php?section=4&menu=5> (25 June 2003).

38. Library of Congress Country Studies, "Agnosticism/Atheism Religion in the Former Czechoslovakia," *2003 Report on Religious Liberty in Czech Republic* (Washington, D.C.: Federal Research Division, World Information, 2003), <http://atheism.about.com/library/world/AJ/bl_CzechReligion.htm>, (24 June 2004).

39. "St. Joseph's Day," *Czech Village Association*, Cedar Rapids, <http://czechvillage.homestead.com/homepage.html>, (24 June 2004).

40. Sayers, 169-70. "Germans had their own schools, universities, press, theatres, and other institutions. . ." This was based on the Language Law of 1920 which permitted ethnic minorities to use their own language in all official capacities.

41. Ibid., 168-170. "Side by side with tensions of class, interwar Czechoslovakia was driven by fault lines of ethnicity."

42. Václav Havel, *Address on the occasion of the conferment of the Nuremberg International Human Rights, Nuremberg, Federal Republic of Germany, 17 September 1995*. "Along with the Munich dictate, the Nuremberg Laws came to my country, too. The flaming synagogues in Liberec and other towns in the Czech

borderlands on the so-called Kristallnacht were a logical outcome of that. Tens of thousands of our citizens, particularly Jews, fled in terror to the interior which was still somewhat safer at the time."<http://old.hrad.cz/president/Havel/speeches/1995/1709_uk.html>, (10 June 2004).

43. Katharina Eisch, "Memory and Identity in Nowhereland. An Ethnographic Study of Non-expelled Germans in the Czech-German Borderlands," *Forced Migration and Displacement: Causes, Consequences, and Responses*, A Multidisciplinary International Conference University of Bath, 12-15 September 2002, <http://staff.bath.ac.uk/mlssaw/fm_conference/abstr.htm> (24 June 2004).

44. Sayer, 240-1. See also The Economist Print Edition, 15 August 2004, *The Benes Decrees: A Spectre Over Central Europe*, <http://www.economist.com/world/europe/displayStory.cfm?story_id=1284252> (25 June 2004).

45. Ivan Klíma, *My Merry Mornings* (London & New York: Readers International Inc., 1985), 32.

46. Ibid, 41-61, 79-83, 115-130.

47. Hampl, 247-8.

48. Havel, 93-96.

49. James VanHise,"Civilian Resistance in Czechoslovakia," *Fragments*. A more detailed account of the passive resistance activities is summarized in the self-published magazine and website.<http://www.fragmentsweb.org/TXT2/czechotx.html> (26 June 2004).

50. Havel, 93-6.

51. Eva Hoffman. *Exit Into History: A Journey Through the New Eastern Europe* (New York: Penguin Books, USA, Inc.,1984), 163. ". . . the citizens of Czechoslovakia were required to believe and pretend they were free, when they were effectively enslaved; that is, they were supposed to live a lie—and an imperative to live a lie sucks sense out of all activity."

REFERENCES

Sala, Joanne, ed. *Czech Proverbs*. Iowa City: Penciled Press, 1994.

Barnes, Jim and Laurie Barnes, "The Czech Spiritual Landscape in the Post-Communist Era," *East-West Church & Ministry Report*, Spring 1996, 6-8. <http://www.samford.edu/groups/global/ewcmreport/articles/ew06205.htm>

Bradatan, Cristina. *Suicide Before and After the Fall of Communism in an Eastern European Society* (for Pennsylvania State University), Oxford, Ohio: Havighurst Center, Russian and Post-Soviet Studies at Miami University (undated). <http://casnov1.cas.muohio.edu/havighurstcenter/papers/bradatan.pdf>

Conway, Francis, and Patrick Box all, *Support for Small Municipalities in the Czech Republic*, Washington, D.C.: The Urban Institute, SAID Project, 1994, iii and 1-3. <http://www.dec.org/pdf_docs/PNACC514.pdf>

Czech Village of Iowa, ed. *St. Joseph's Day*. Czech Village Association. Cedar Rapid. <http://czechvillage.homestead.com/homepage.html>

Eisch, Katharina, "Memory and Identity in Nowhereland. An Ethnographic Study of Non-expelled Germans in the Czech-German Borderlands," *Forced Migration and Displacement: Causes, Consequences, and Responses*, A Multidisciplinary International Conference University of Bath. 12-15 September 2002. <http://staff.bath.ac.uk/mlssaw/fm_conference/abstr.htm>

Hampl, Patricia. *A Romantic Education*. Boston & New York: Houghton Mifflin Company, 1981.

Hartunian, Ceeroosh, M.D, interview by author, Manhattan Beach, CA. (6 April 2000).

Havel, Václav, *Address on the occasion of the conferment of the Nuremberg International Human Rights*. Nuremberg, Federal Republic of Germany, *17*

September 1995. <http://old.hrad.cz/president/Havel/speeches/ 1995/1709_uk.html>

Havel, Václav. *Disturbing the Peace.* New York: Alfred A. Knopf, 1990.

Hilliard, Asa. *World literacy rates, 2002-2003.* <http://www.ideal-group.org/ Literacy_Rates.htm>

Hoffman, Eva. *Exit Into History: A Journey Through the New Eastern Europe.* New York: Penguin Books USA, Inc., 1994.

Klíma, Ivan. *My Merry Mornings.* London & New York: Readers International Inc., 1985.

Library of Congress Country Studies, "Agnosticism/Atheism Religion in the Former Czechoslovakia," *2003 Report on Religious Liberty in Czech Republic,* Washington, D.C.: Federal Research Division, World Information, 2003. <http://atheism.about.com/library/world/AJ/bl_CzechReligion.htm> (24 June 2004).

Lovely Recipes, ed. *Semolina Info Tips and Information.* <http://www.lovelyrecipes.com/cooking-tip.php?recipeid=2687>

Město Jablonec nad Nisou, *Town History* (author unknown). Městsky úřad Jablonec nad Nisou, Czech Republic. <http://www.mestojablonec.cz/mesto/ historie_en.php> (20 June 2004).

NJMS National Tuberculosis Center, "Brief History of Tuberculosis," New Jersey, 1996. <http//www.umdnj.edu/~ntbcweb/history.htm> (28 June 2004).

New River Notes, ed. (undated). *A Wonderful Spring! Thompson's Bromine Arsenic Water Springs in Ashe County, N.C.* Eli Barker. <http://www.ls.net/~newriver/ nc/heal1887.htm>

Radio Prague - the International Service of Czech Radio. *Radio Prague - 65 years.* <http://www.radio.cz/en/html/65_clouds.html>

Radio Prague Internet. *Jablonec nad Nisou.* <http://archiv.radio.cz/mapa/ more.phtml?mesto=8>

Rovensko pod Troskami. *základní informace.* <http://www.rovensko.cz>

Sayer, Derek. *The Coasts of Bohemia.* Princeton: Princeton University Press, 1998.

Seznam míst v království Českém. (author unknown). Circa 1912. Hapsburg publication (city unknown).

Statistický Lexikon Obcí v Republice Československé. Vydán ministerstvem vnitra a Státním úřadem statistickým. "1. Země Česká." Praha, 1934.

"Spas," *Czech Republic: Ministry of Foreign Affairs,* 2002. <http://www.czech.cz/ index.php?section=4&menu=5> (25 June 2003).

The Economist Print Edition, 15 August 2004, *The Benes Decrees: A Spectre Over Central Europe,* <http://czechvillage.homestead.com/homepage.html>

The Embassy of the Czech Republic, *Religion,* <http://www.mzv.cz/washington/ general/general.htm#Religion>

The Evangelical Church of Czech Brethren, *History,* Ecumenical Council of Churches in the Czech Republic, 2001. <http://www.ekumenickarada.cz/ erceng/cce.html>

"Total Mobilization, Resistance, and the Holocaust," *German Culture*. <http://www.germanculture.com.ua/library/history/bl_holocaust.htm> (23 June 2004).

Valach, Tony, "Vera Masa Biographical Sketch," *Tucson Czech-Slovak Club Newsletter,* 2004, April. <http://tucsonczechslovak.homestead.com/Newsletter2.html>

VanHise, James, "Civilian Resistance in Czechoslovakia," *Fragments*, <http://www.fragmentsweb.org/TXT2/czechotx.html> (26 June 2004).

Wikipedia, ed. (undated), Protectorate of Bohemia and Moravia, <http://en.wikipedia.org/wiki/Protectorate_of_Bohemia_and_Moravia>

ABOUT THE AUTHORS

Sylvia Welner earned her B.A. in English from UCLA, and her M.A. in Bilingual/Multicultural Studies from California State University, Dominguez Hills. She holds teaching credentials at the elementary and adult education levels, administered and taught bilingual classes for fifteen years, and has published poetry as well as an instructional guide on teaching poetry writing to the bilingual child. She also developed instructional materials for Xerox Corporation, winning international awards for her writing. The current manuscript is grounded, in part, on two trips she made to the Czech Republic, where she investigated sites and localities mentioned in the book.

Kevin G. Welner is an associate professor at the University of Colorado, Boulder School of Education, specializing in educational policy, law, and program evaluation. He is co-director of the CU-Boulder Education in the Public Interest Center (EPIC). His research examines the intersection between education rights litigation and educational opportunity scholarship, and he is author of *Legal Rights, Local Wrongs: When Community Control Collides with Educational Equity* (SUNY Press, 2001). He earned both his J.D. and Ph.D. from UCLA.